Restoring the Paths:
Sexuality for Christian Leaders

Lisa M. Sinclair, DMin, MSN

Restoring the Paths: Sexuality for Christian Leaders

Scripture quotations are from The ESV® Bible (The Holy Bible, English Standard Version®), copyright © 2001 by Crossway, a publishing ministry of Good News Publishers. Used by permission. All rights reserved.

ISBN: 978-1-7341169-7-7

Library of Congress Control Number: pending

Printed in the United States of America

T.A.L.K. Publishing, LLC

talkconsulting.net

Dedication

I am profoundly honored by the missionaries and ministers that have honored me with their stories of sexual grief and pain. I dedicate this book to them, heroes of faith, "those of whom the world was not worthy" (Heb. 11:38).

"Your path led through the sea, your way through the mighty waters, though your footprints were not seen." (Ps. 77:19)

Table of Contents

Foreword

Are you prepared?

The light has shone into a very dark place. A key has opened a box long hidden in the recesses of the Church and the word has escaped is – SEX.

We all probably would agree that conventions regarding sexuality in Western cultures have been changing rapidly and have brought with them the need to consider sexual issues in ways we never considered in the past.

Is there a Christian distinctive in the areas of premarital sex, adultery, pornography usage and sexual abuse? Scientific data suggests that there is not. What a sad fact.

Are there Christians who struggle with their sexual identity or sexual attractions? Of course, some do.

Has the Church historically and currently led the way for the world to see and respond to the Bible's answers for so many of these types of problems? Or, are we stereotyped as being narrowminded and prejudiced and therefore discounted from offering viable solutions? You must answer these questions for yourself.

As Christian leaders, we are expected to have answers and to be able to help those struggling in these and other sexual areas. Dr. Sinclair identifies well the obstacles we face that keep us from doing the best job we can in dealing with these sexual areas both personally and in counseling opportunities. These include issues such as our work ethic, the image we strive to build and maintain, insufficient education and preparation regarding sexuality, the pitfalls of temptations specific to ministry and the limited availability of resources. Using true stories, she helps us see the effects these problems cause in real life. By asking pertinent questions, she helps us to "put on your oxygen mask first, so you can then help the others with whom you are travelling." By offering copious resources, she supplies us with the information we need to close our own personal gaps in this area.

In this book, we are guided by a true expert. I have been blessed to know Lisa for more than 35 years and have seen her walk God's path through the minefields of sexual dysfunction to a place of healing and victory. She has studied this area thoroughly for her Doctor of Ministry (DMin) dissertation. She has been involved personally in many roles of Christian leadership and counseled many as they struggle in these areas. She has taught Christians locally, nationally and internationally on the same topics that she now shares with us. Most importantly, her suggestions and conclusions are all Scripturally based. What an opportunity we have in these pages to have our own sexuality aligned more perfectly to God's design and be more prepared to shine that light into a broken and needy world.

Gloria Halverson M.D.
President, Christian Medical and Dental Association
June 2019

Acknowledgments

God has set the lonely in families. I am so thankful for the women who have shown me what it means to be a woman, some of whom are already receiving their reward. My mother-in-law, Opal Virnig, modeled beauty, hospitality and creativity to me. My mother taught me to laugh. Ruth Cloninger prayed healing for me that extended to the "cellular level." Colleen Cameranesi and Bonnie Thomas believed in me. My daughters, Elisabeth, Rebekah, Kara and Lori teach me how to love and nurture. My granddaughters Ella, Teagan, Hazel, Bailey and Daizy show me joy and teach me to dance.

God has fathered me well. I have learned discipline, structure, a love for the lost and a passion for the Word of God from Robertson McQuilkin, Bill Larkin, Terry Hulbert and Stuart Briscoe. My son, Luke, and my grandson, Kaiden, bless me with their masculine kindness. My sons-in-law model persevering love and hope--what it means "when a man loves a woman" in our world today.

Our friends have done marriage "work" with us in the most perilous times and in daily commitment. I am grateful for their care, vulnerability, perseverance and grace: Kathy and Phil, Roselyn and Virgil, Jan and Tim, Karen and Dave, and Glor and Paul.

We have been blessed with good therapists that have helped us unravel the wounds of the past and see the way forward in our marriage. Thank you to Herb, Bill, Hal and Lori. Thanks to OA, FA, Al-Anon and Celebrate Recovery.

It has been my joy to work with Living Waters. I am grateful for the ministry and care from the national staff including Andrew

Comiskey, Dean Greer, Ann Armstrong, Abbey Foard and Daniel Delgado--along with my "trusted companions" in our local group, John, Mike, Talva, Paul, Greg, Libby, Sue, Victoria, Ellen, Jill and JoLanda. I'm so glad to be at Eastbrook Church and under the ministry of Pastors Matt Erickson and Ruth Carver.

Finally, I thank my husband, Paul. We celebrated our 40th anniversary during the completion of this book. It would not have come into existence without his steadfast love and courageous journey to wholeness. I thank God that we continue to discover the ancient paths together.

Introduction

"Do not move the ancient boundary which your fathers have set."
(Proverbs 22:28)

My heart broke as I listened to the story of a recently divorced woman. Leah[1] finally left her husband. Her family and church were shattered. Her story reveals the urgent need for help in the church.

> *I was a prostitute in our marriage. I remember the day that I started feeling like a body on the bed. It wasn't mutual. It wasn't about connecting. It was about demand--using my body to satisfy his wants and needs no matter the cost. I didn't know how to leave. I was alone and trapped. I had "made my bed" and had to " lie in it." I was obligated as a submissive wife and as a pastor's wife. It was my duty to satisfy his needs so that he wouldn't end up in porn or lusting after other women. It was my job to protect his ministry from ruin. When I expressed a desire for sex to be mutual, I was told that it was my fault that I didn't feel connected. I was broken and needed to be fixed. I had issues. I needed to try harder. And, I believed it. Everywhere I went I heard about how amazing he was--so, I owned it and wore it. I promoted the storyline that I was this broken, damaged woman and he was this amazing man who stayed with me when most men would leave. I spent most of our married life seeing doctors and counselors trying to get fixed. Each time that I let myself be a body on a bed, I betrayed myself and didn't want to be in my skin afterward. When my husband told me about the affair, he blamed me--I had driven him into her arms. She wanted him. She saw him as great. I didn't want to be a prostitute anymore, but when I refused that, he found someone else.*

Leah explained that she felt a glimmer of light and healing when she told her spiritual director that God hadn't answered her years of prayers to be healed. Her director replied, *"Maybe He hasn't healed you because you aren't broken."*

In 2010, I completed my dissertation for my Doctor of Ministry. My subject focused on the healing experience of marital sexual betrayal in North American missionary women. Through the qualitative research process of extensive interviewing, I realized that the themes that emerged went far beyond married North American missionary women. Because of interest around this topic and strong exhortations as to the need for it, I decided to turn my dissertation into a readable book. As I started to work on it, I realized that it was like starting in the middle of a mystery. A foundation needed to be laid long before I could address the awful pain of sexual betrayal.

There are several good books on sexuality, and they serve as prequels to this book.[2] But Christian leaders face enormous challenges in their theological, practical and personal understanding of sexuality and they are my focused audience.

We live in times of rapid change. Things that we have held to be true are being swept away, "deconstructed,"[3] sometimes dramatically, sometimes imperceptibly. We are left to question what has happened. What is right? What is truth? Our post-modern culture brings with it a tsunami of emptiness and normlessness with real resistance to any guidelines for decision-making around behavior or values.

There is a riptide pull of legislation and media that promotes sexuality as an individual domain. What is right is what feels right. My individual choices are just that--mine! If there are ramifications external to me, well then, they are your problem and you will need to deal with them.

The ancient boundary markers of Scripture, of a Judeo-Christian cultural foundation, of the faith of our fathers, have been moved—often so far that we have trouble excavating them.

How are we as followers of Jesus to stand true to Him? What does it even mean? We have lost the metanarrative of God's redeeming love for the world and, too often, we are bobbing around like flotsam and jetsam, irrelevant to the current questions, issues, and profound needs that surround us. We are reactive rather than initiating and prophetic.

Our lack of biblical literacy and understanding of both the history of the church and general ecclesiology have left us vulnerable to the powerful climate shifts of our culture without a strong anchor. Without biblical authority and Church authority, we are prey to our own whims and desires that are ever-changing.

Our own brokenness and sinfulness combine with our ignorance and isolation. We may gradually begin to question our old values, "Has God really said?" Our personal issues of sexual abuse or sexual sin, of same-sex attraction or gender confusion and of unmet intimacy needs combine with tremendous external pressures to potentially shipwreck our lives and ministries. Our ability to minister to others can founder in our desire to be compassionate and tolerant.

This book is an attempt to dive for the ancient markers, identify them and provide indicators for us as Christian leaders to help navigate these turbulent seas. It is written to help us understand our current cultural context and our unique ministry challenges. It provides helps for growth and healing in our own sexuality as well as implications for church education.

It is my prayer that it will be a valuable resource for you.

Part One: The unique challenges of ministry sexuality

But my people have forgotten me; they make offerings to false gods; they made them stumble in their ways, in the ancient roads, and to walk into side roads, not the highway. (Jeremiah 18:15)

Christian leaders face many stresses. We have influence and a position of power over others. Our roles are diverse—pastors and priests, apostles and missionaries, teachers, spiritual directors, mentors, counselors and administrators. We are male, female, young, old and represent all ethnicities and denominations. Our challenges may vary according to our demographic and position, but Christian leadership impacts our sexuality. And our sexuality impacts our leadership.

This section of the book will identify some of the unique challenges that leaders face. We will look at challenges that come:

- from the nature of the call
- from image building and image maintaining
- from the lack of education and preparation in human and personal sexuality
- from the increased exposure to sexual temptations in ministry
- from the limited availability of safe help and resources

Chapter 1: The Call

Abigail and her husband were missionaries in Africa. She and her husband lived a performance-based Christianity. They were missionary poster children. Her painful story describes them.

> On the outside, we were great missionaries--working with a hard, unreached people group, doing and working really great performance-wise, building churches, planting—doing. We were great language learners, checking off all the things on our to-do list of good missionaries. We were living that. But on the inside? We were crumbling as a couple.

Abigail and her husband had to leave the mission field because of his serial unfaithfulness with national women. They returned at great cost.

To be called to ministry is to be called to an honored position that assumes high ethical behavior and personal holiness. People look up to those in ministry, and often turn to them first in times of crisis and need. Christian leaders live in a fishbowl, surrounded by high expectations. You are always "on." What you say and what you do is under public scrutiny and evaluation. This constant state of observation includes your loved ones, e.g. your spouse's involvement and attitude and your children's obedience and engagement.

Your work ethic is affirmed by your congregation or organization, often to the detriment of yourself and your family. The group may provide many forms of verbal and nonverbal affirmation for the leader that works long hours, is always available by phone, text, or email and is always willing to respond to crises of all kinds. Leaders may say, "First God, then family, then church" but practically, you can live out a kind of idolatry to work. Your work or ministry controls your time, your leisure and your priorities. Your own needs and self-care are often subservient to the call. Your marriage and family needs and care may be minimized or neglected secondary to ministry.

The "call" is no longer to God, but rather to the task. It no longer involves personal discipleship and deeper abiding in Christ. It no longer is understood in the context of intimate connection with a few close others. As Emmy, a missionary to South America for 19 of her 20 years of marriage, said, *"We were 'workaholics'—we were more connected to work and ministry than to each other."*

The call to ministry and leadership is a unique challenge for the Christian leader. It is an essential foundation, and yet can be used to camouflage personal inadequacy and insecurity, or to disconnect from personal and relational wounds. The call may turn into appearance management—looking holy, looking busy, looking successful—versus the developing reality of slow sanctification.

Reflection: *How have you experienced and understood your call? How has it affected your use of time or your development of work and personal boundaries? What are the implications of the call on your own experience of sexuality?*

Chapter 2: Maintaining the Image

Clothilde was a pastor's wife for more than 25 years. She ironically noted that although most people know about PKs (pastor's kids), they don't seem to be aware of PWs (pastor's wives). Her features were tight as she described her husband's work persona.

> *My husband always spoke in a different voice in public. He pronounced "God" differently, he smiled more and gave more eye contact. He used physical touch regularly and laughed often. He was generous and attentive. But with me, he was "dead." In our home, he was distant, distracted, exhausted and uninvolved.*

Image building and image maintaining are closely tied to the call. Earnest appreciation of the call can lead to performance orientation. Because of the public nature of the ministry role, performance orientation can lead to a sense of need to maintain a certain image. It is unfortunate that many leaders develop a sort of ministry mask, a kind of persona that doesn't match the true self. One missionary wife called this the "plastic fantastic."

Success is measured by numbers of converts, baptisms, churches planted, blog hits, sermons heard, or the number of people helped. It becomes very important to protect reputation and to be seen as successful. Vulnerability, true vulnerability—not the kind that shares from the pulpit to win sympathy and support—is experienced as a weakness instead of a strength. True accountability and help are not sought in difficulty because the minister/leader "should" be the expert, the good one, the holy one. Transparency and integrity can be sacrificed to maintain the image.

The leader can begin to believe his or her own press. Insecurity, inadequacy, ignorance, failure and besetting sin become submerged under the false image of the high-performing minister. Often it is the spouse and family that recognize the mask first and fight against its harmful effects. The minister, however, may spiritualize "false self" behavior and shut down all family protest, justifying the need for ministry behavior. This phenomenon is fed by a lack of privacy and the family being on display all the time.

In between the God-created true self and the false self of the public persona lies the ability to live in integrity or in secrecy and deceit. Here a dark world can develop where stress, loneliness, isolation, sexual frustration, inadequacy and feelings of anger and blame fuel patterns of sexual sin and release. This shadow land harbors tremendous energy that enables unrealistic work schedules and intensive output. It also harbors forces of evil and destruction, for Satan roars like a lion, seeking to devour—to steal, kill and destroy (1 Peter 5:8; John 10:10). The "naked and unashamed" of Scripture (Gen. 2:25) becomes cloaked with protectiveness and shame.

God desires truth in our innermost being (Ps. 51:6). In leadership, integrity around sexuality can exact a heavy toll. Historically, sexual sin has been viewed and treated as the worst sin. Homosexuality has been vilified. Pedophilia is considered unforgivable. Any confession or search for help on the part of the Christian leader or family may cause public outcry, hurtful publicity, or loss of job with no chance of future professional ministry. There are concomitant disastrous effects on the family and the church/mission and its work.

Most people in ministry lack a strong support system and routine disciplines of regular confession and meaningful accountability. It is no surprise that sexual issues are hidden behind the mask of ministry.

Reflection: *Do you have a public persona? Would those closest to you be able to describe your false self? Has a kind of dark world developed in the schism between your true and false self? Have you shared with anyone what is truly going on in your heart?*

Chapter 3: Inadequate Preparation

Jim's parents never taught him anything about sexuality. As a boy, he learned what he could by looking at pornography and feeling terrible shame about his emerging sexual curiosity. He didn't feel that he could talk to anyone about it. He tells his story with regret and longing:

> I was about 12 when my dad asked me if I wanted to go for a walk. This wasn't normal—he never asked me to go for a walk! I wondered what was coming but was glad for time with my Dad. After a while we sat down. He said, "So, do you have any questions?" I didn't know what he was talking about, and said, "No." That was the end of my sex education!

Jim thought that marriage would "cure" his pornography use, compulsive masturbation, and fantasy life. It didn't. These were areas that no one discussed when he went to seminary. The increased stress of ministry life brought increased use of sexual "medicators" until he was discovered and publicly disciplined. Now he wonders, *"What would have happened if my family spoke openly about sex? If I'd learned anything in school, or church, or the seminary? Would we have had to go through all of this?"* He described his whole sexual journey as very lonely.

Ministers are ill-prepared to face their context of heightened sexual pressures. Churches are not reflecting Scripture with regular teaching about sexuality through sermons or adult and youth education. Seminaries are only starting to address the need for preparation in the face of rampant allegations, situations of abuse, and "moral failure" in the professional religious community. Mission agencies and mission training institutes tend to be aware of the needs, but often are ill-equipped financially, professionally and in terms of time commitment to address these needs. There is a lack of ongoing continuing education for ministers in areas of sexuality and its current challenges. There may be support groups for sexual issues or brokenness, or referrals to specialists, but not much matter of fact, normalized, every-day teaching.

The questions below are just a few examples of areas of needed preparation. Christian leaders need theological and personal preparation to respond to the questions and issues that are generated today.

- What does it mean to be created male and female in the image of God? Why did God do this?
- Why am I male or female? Is it ok to change that? Why or why not?
- Does God set a pattern for heterosexual monogamous marriage? And if so, why?
- Why does He seem to treat polygamy so casually in Scripture?
- What's wrong with same sex unions or marriage if we love and are committed to each other?
- How are we to handle our sexual desires? How do we handle same-sex attraction? How do we handle premarital attraction and desire? How do we handle extramarital attraction and desire? What about paraphilias?
- How do we address the Church legacy of viewing sex as bad and judging sexual sin as the worst of sins? Of demonizing those with same sex attraction or gender confusion? Of all the publicized hypocrisy?
- What about masturbation?
- If God created us and says that sex is good, why shouldn't we express that? Is traditional heterosexual monogamous marriage a cultural concept, or is it biblical and permanent?

- How do we handle differing levels of sexual interest in marriage? Inhibited sexual desire? Lack of mutual fulfillment?
- What specific sexual practices are OK, and which are not?
- How do we heal from our sexual wounds, abuse and trauma from our family of origin?
- How do we evaluate and cope with the myriad of sexual messages that we receive daily?
- Was Jesus sexual?
- How do we apply Scriptural principles to today's complicated context? Are there guidelines to interpret Scripture?
- How do we understand and explain the theological differences and stances about sexuality across denominations?
- How do we deal with feelings of attraction in ministry situations? How do we respond to seductive invitations?
- How do we defend ourselves, our family and our people from sexual predators, pain and sin?

We could go on and on. If there isn't adequate emotional and sexuality preparation for the leader, there also isn't ongoing mentoring, coaching and accountability for us as sexual persons. If we as leaders are ill-prepared, then we are clearly ill-equipped to address the needs of our community and world.

Reflection: *How were you prepared for the unique sexual challenges of Christian leadership? What areas of preparation did you need and not receive? What would you have liked and how could it have been provided? How has your lack of sexuality preparation been a challenge to you as a Christian leader?*

Chapter 4: Exposure to Temptation

Ellie and her husband served in an isolated area of Africa. They were redeployed to the field after a 2-year restoration process for her husband's pornography use. In retrospect, she realizes how naïve they had been about prevalent sexual temptation on the field—the polygamy, the expectation of sexual sin by the nationals, the use of sex for favors, the nudity and frequent sexual rituals. She said,

> I'm so angry at Satan and how he hones right in on sexuality as a means of destroying marriages and ministries. I don't want to use spiritual warfare to excuse anyone's sinful choices, but men in particular need extra prayer for a wall of protection around their sexuality and for strength in their inner man to stand firm against the pull of various temptations of their eyes and minds and bodies. But I also believe that for every temptation there is a way out and my husband wasn't looking very hard to find it.

The intensity of sexual temptation is often surprising to leaders. Remember that people in ministry tend to be overworked and not attending to their own personal needs for rest, retreat, reflection and recreation.[1] This puts them in a position of vulnerability to sexual temptation.

Ministry leaders may be naïve about temptation, believing that obedience to the call will protect them from sexual temptation rather than realizing that this is a vulnerability frequently attacked.

Leaders also tend to be emotionally ill-prepared for the stress of ministry. One minister's wife told me that she thought that part of what led her husband to sexual sin was his *"naivete about emotional boundaries, about the dynamics of relating such as transference and countertransference.*" He was seen in good ways as father and counselor and mate or son, but he was also seen as the authority figure or male who had wounded in the past. He entered into roles and expectations and reactions that were more about someone else than about him. Similarly, his own relationship with congregants was unhealthy due to him meeting needs through them for his own unresolved hurts.[2]

The codependent need to be needed has paved the way for many a fall. It is not unusual for ministers and leaders to respond to a call with unexplored past wounding that has left them insecure. They are driven to workaholism, perfectionism, achievement and performance—all in an attempt to gain approval. The longing for affirmation is easily sexualized.

Many organizations utilize psychiatric evaluations and personal inventories to try and determine if there are preexisting issues that drive leaders to public ministry. These instruments are not perfect, and their results can be misinterpreted or lightly esteemed, but they are very helpful in the hands of a professional consultant. They are also expensive and time-consuming. Other organizations rely on personal interviews and references. These can be skewed to hide unaddressed personality and sexual issues that wreak havoc later in the stress and warfare that characterize Christian leadership.

When people are in crisis or experience a tragedy, they often turn to clergy before any other professional. These situations of grief and pain are very personal, and a deep intimacy can be forged between the victim and the minister. In our oversexualized culture, it is not unusual for someone to sexualize his or her pain or grief and to offer sexual intimacy as a way of meeting need or expressing appreciation. Leaders frequently provide comfort by holding a hand, putting an arm around a hurting person, hugging people in and out of church. They need to be aware of the impact of their use of touch on their congregants as well as aware of their own vulnerability to sexual responsiveness through touch. Personal boundaries and accountability systems need to be clearly established and understood.

Many leaders follow the open door or window policy for their personal offices, so that they are never in total privacy. Others follow the "Billy Graham policy" of a man not being alone with a woman in a car. These tend to be superficial behavioral boundaries that can be very helpful, but do not address internal needs and drives that might cause a person to be vulnerable to temptation. Policies such as these are easily circumvented. If your organization has such policies, it is necessary to explain their rationale.[3]

Accountability relationships are easily manipulated. I remember a leader ironically referring to Wesley's accountability questions and to the final question that Chuck Swindoll added, "Have you just lied to me?"[4] Someone who will lie in an accountability relationship will lie in response to these questions, but this doesn't negate the importance of accountability. Rather, it encourages us to be attentive to the Holy Spirit's leading with a healthy dose of skepticism. As Jeremiah 17:9 reminds us, "The heart is deceitful above all things and beyond cure. Who can understand it?"

People in ministry tend to depend on the internet for their work research and preparation. There they are exposed to the "AAA engine" in anonymous, affordable and accessible pornography and romantic fantasy that can quickly addict.[5]

Emotional affairs are prevalent in ministry. Male and female leaders are isolated because of their position and can be emotionally distant and disconnected from their spouse or support network due to stress and busyness. Malenda, a missionary wife, noted with obvious shame that she had had an emotional affair.

I was so lonely. I felt neglected. The work always came first and was way more important than I was. Our sex life was infrequent and mechanical. My language instructor found me fascinating. We met for several hours a day. My husband knew about it, but he felt that it was important that I learn the language—and maybe it kept me out of his hair, I don't know. Then, on home ministry, one of our supporters was so impressed with me. He wanted to know what I thought and felt about just about everything. He found me beautiful. It was only by God's grace that I didn't commit physical adultery.

Missionaries may be exposed to easy and frequent offers of prostitution or free sex. This can be a cultural way of honoring the leader. There may be fantasies about how polygamy works - and a secret fantasy to try it out can develop. Missionaries are exposed to different standards of nudity. Without realizing it, they can begin to internalize these values.

Western culture increasingly provides nudity and sexually explicit behaviors on regular media sources. This reflects Western promiscuity, erosion of norms and an increasing sense of sexual rights and entitlement that may gradually erode a leader's boundaries and titillate the imagination.

We in ministry need to be aware of our own sexual needs and desires. We need to have a realistic appraisal of our temptations and figure out a plan of defense. Otherwise, we are sitting ducks for sexual sin that will violate our own call, the trust of our people and will deeply wound our spouse, family, and team.

Reflection: *Think over your own ministry experience. What have been your most difficult sexual and emotional temptations? How did you handle them? Do you have an accountability system in effect and how well is it working? What do you wish you had known about sexual temptation in the ministry to protect yourself? What can you do now?*

Chapter 5: Limited Availability of Help and Resources

Jeannette is the wife of a megachurch pastor. She and her husband both admit that their marriage has not been easy. Their transparency has provided a safe place for their large congregation to admit and address marital and family pain. But Jeannette and her husband have had a hard time finding help for themselves. They are known everywhere they go, and the best counselors often tend to be people in their own sphere of influence. If and when they find someone who is safe in terms of confidentiality, will that person understand the extraordinary stresses of leading a megachurch, and the associated stresses on their marriage and their sexuality?

Just as there is a lack of preparation, there also is a lack of safe help and resources available to those in ministry leadership. This is because of the public nature of leadership and the reality that confidentiality is easily breached with harmful ramifications. It is also due to a lack of awareness of the unique challenges of Christian leadership. If the need is not realized, then help and resources are not developed and made available. Missionaries serving in more remote contexts have an even greater need and less availability of resources.[1]

Below are some examples of common areas of need for resourcing that I have discovered in both my research and private practice with Christian leaders.

- How do I learn more about sex and what is physiologically normal? What is good?

- When I know and feel my sexual needs and desires, how do I express them to my spouse and teach my partner to meet them? What if our needs and desires are different? How do we reconcile these differences? What does it mean to be "one flesh"?
- How do I handle my sexual needs as a single? Is masturbation OK? How far can I go on a date? Is heavy petting or mutual masturbation OK as long as there is no intercourse?
- How do I teach my children about sex?
- How do I find resources to help me teach and preach on sex?
- Where do I find trustworthy, Christ-honoring, counselors?
- Is it wrong for a Christian couple to see a sex therapist? How do we find one?
- What do we do with our own disordered desires? How do I handle same sex attraction?
- I hate my body. How do I get healing about that?
- I hate sex—what do I do about that?
- I think about sex all the time. What do I do about that?
- How do I help my children or teammates with sexual problems?
- How do we deal with our own sexual failures? How do we forgive in marriage and build trust after betrayal?
- How do we work with people that are attractive to us, or are attracted to us? How do we handle mutual attraction?

There are all kinds of personal and marital sexual difficulties that cry out for assistance but are suffered in silence.[2] Often, leaders simply long for a safe place to discuss all the confidential information that they possess. They need a safe place to process their difficult counseling situations. They need safe resources for their own personal, marital and family issues. Because they serve in a public role and because their work is confidential, they must be very careful what they share and with whom they share.

Often, the resources or counseling available (especially sex therapy) is offered from a secular perspective. Available help and resources must run the test of trustworthiness, but it is very difficult to determine that without risking exposure.[3]

Reflection: *What resources have you needed that weren't available because you are a minister/leader? What do you wish you had access to? What resources are available through your church or organization? Do you have a reference list of reliable counselors and treatment centers? Have you ever experienced (or been a part of) a breach of confidentiality?*

Part One has identified some of the unique challenges of Christian leadership in terms of sexuality. Now we will take an outward look at our surrounding culture.

Part Two: Sexuality Today

"In those days there was no king in Israel. Everyone did what was right in his own eyes." (Judges 21:25)

In this section, I will address briefly our current historical and cultural context and provide my own story. Our culture is changing rapidly. Each of us needs to ask God for wisdom and guidance to do careful and ongoing analysis to understand current issues, trends, motivations, and expectations so that we can minister effectively to the world around us.

Chapter 6: My story

And such were some of you. But you were washed, you were sanctified, you were justified in the name of the Lord Jesus Christ and by the Spirit of our God. (1 Cor. 6:11)

I came to maturity during the sexual revolution. When I was a little girl, I delighted in dancing and wearing lipstick and dressing up. But gradually, almost imperceptibly, my childhood innocence and pleasure in being a girl dissolved as I absorbed the sexual sin around me. By puberty, any hint of sex frightened me even as it gave me a strange sense of power.

My mother struggled with mental illness and alcoholism and her behavior was often hypersexual. At age 6, I lost a protective shield when my father left and then died suddenly when I was 8. My brother and I accompanied my mother on her evening trips to bars. She would dance and strip on the tabletop until the police were called to remove her. We ran the streets when she was gone or incarcerated, vulnerable to its dangers and evil. She engaged in casual and frightening relationships, bringing men home who intended us all harm. We lived on the edges of her madness and tried to keep her and ourselves safe.

By the time that I was 8, I hated wearing dresses and wore my brother's way-too-big clothes. I pretended I was a boy. When my step-cousins and I engaged in playing house or doctor, I was always the boy, always the tough one. Between the ages of 10 and 12, I was molested, as too many are, in the unsafe world of fatherlessness, unsupervised care and latchkey kids.

I came to Christ when I was 17, and while I never regained my child-like unselfconscious delight in my body, I did believe that

God made me and loved me. I never questioned that I was "made" to be a
girl--and my culture and social group affirmed that.

I went to college in 1970, the height of the sexual revolution. I thought that I would be a philosophy/religion major. This was my plan to grow in my faith. We studied "situation ethics"[1] and my professors explained that to be a Christian meant to behave according to what was the most loving in any given moment. I started to live that out, sleeping with needy or troubled men, as if "bedroom evangelism" would bring some kind of healing or good to them--or to me.

By the time I was 25, I had been sexually abused, experienced incest and had been raped. I had married an unbeliever thinking that, somehow, I could save him. I had aborted my first baby. I was a single parent with no idea of how to raise a little girl. My marriage was ending in divorce and I was illegitimately pregnant.

I reaped so much pain through sexuality, my sin and multiple others' sins against me! As I placed my baby for adoption, I learned about obedience. I learned that God loved me so much that He gave His only son for me. I learned that my actions had consequences. I learned that God wanted to transform my legacy of abuse, self-hatred, body shame and sin into an integrated woman of hope and joy.

I found out that Christians go to church! I learned that Scripture is God's love letter to us. When I married again in 1979 with the counsel and permission of my church, my godly husband and I knew the call of God on our lives. We were called to the neediest places.

We went to seminary to become missionaries. When we had inevitable struggles, I returned to the old default messages of my youth: I was "ugly, fat and stupid." Clearly, I was the problem and the one to blame. I had not experienced a conservative Christian upbringing as my husband had and I didn't know anything about the "religious sexual shame"[2] that had contributed to molding him.

It took many years for my husband to reveal his lifelong struggles with sexual addiction issues. I experienced such a deep betrayal-- as if God had departed from my life. We had given everything to serve Him on the mission field. Why hadn't He protected us? Really, why hadn't He protected me? After long years of recovery, we now can share God's healing work in our lives. We realize, as a friend once remarked to us, "From our deepest woundings our deepest healings come."

I tell you my story because like the apostle Paul, I know that I am the foremost of sinners (1 Tim. 1:12-16). I have experienced God's great mercy and lavished grace. He has put me into service as an example of His love and faithfulness.

Maybe some of you are like us, world-scarred and broken, struggling towards wholeness. Whether this has been your experience or not, you will have colleagues and teammates whose woundedness will complicate your working relationships. But whatever our personal or close associates' experience, our congregations will be hungry for our understanding, grace and truth, and wisdom and counsel.

I am grateful that I was born in 1952 and not 2020. Today, I would have thought that I was a boy in a girl's body. I would have been affirmed and socialized in this. Perhaps I would have taken steps to avoid puberty, bound my breasts or hidden my menstruation. I would have joined myself to the boys' world and rejected that which was female. I might have gone on to have "upper body" surgery and removed hated organs of my femininity. I might have started on hormone therapy to change my sex characteristics. My sexual desires would have been channeled to whatever seemed good at the time. My whole life would have revolved around my sexuality and my experience of it, making it what I thought it ought to be.

Just imagining this is frightening. I might have been so disenchanted through abuse and deception that I took an easier path to another divorce, or unfaithfulness, or same sex relationships. Instead, I have been on the excruciating and glorious path of being made into Christlikeness.

I have learned that my sexuality is an integral part of my identity. I am created female, and this is no accident. My past gender dis-ease, my body dysmorphia,[3] my various and changing sexual needs and desires are all part of me, all part of what is submitted to the Lordship of Christ when I become His. This journey has included surrendering, counseling, mistakes, failures, heartbreak, loneliness, misunderstandings, confusion and fighting the good fight of faith. It has meant believing and hoping for what I do not see or feel. It has meant trusting God's plan for me and His continual loving involvement in my life.

It is good that I am woman. It is good that I am feminine. It is good that I long for relationship and intimacy. It is good that I am gifted as I am. All of this is part of God's process of discipling and sanctifying me.

God has mothered and fathered me through the Church, and I am so grateful for the healthy men and women who have loved me and my husband and taught us to accept who we are made to be. We have been blessed to be part of Desert Stream Living Waters[4] and to have a fellowship of men and women that are committed to the journey of surrender and obedience, to following the rhythm of the Cross.

Reflection: *How has your family and church background affected your understanding of sexuality, gender and intimacy? Take time to journal thoughts, feelings, and memories of your own sexual journey as you read this book.*

Chapter 7: Historical Review

We all are aware of the historical shift around us. The ancient boundary markers have been moved with contraception, cohabitation, decreasing marriage rates, reproductive technology, LGBTQ+ affirmation, homosexual marriage and permissive fluidity of gender identity. Access to therapeutic counseling for a desire to change sexual orientation/identity or gender is now restricted. We don't know the outcome of these changes; we are riding big waves that can be exhilarating to some and terrifying to others.

With all the good of feminism, contraception, reproductive technology and surgery to correct defects or injuries, a dark side has emerged and taken root. Sexuality is a choice, not a given. Sexual preference, orientation, identity and behavior are rights, not responsibilities. Now we can choose if we are physiologically male or female and whether our gender matches our physiology or is one of an increasing number of variations. Now we can live according to our feelings, needs and desires. If I want or need fulfillment from another, whatever gender, or from myself, I am free and encouraged to meet those needs, and to expect, seek and demand what is my right.

"Anomie" is the word for living in a state without norms, limits or guidelines. We intuitively know that children need structure. Many of us have experienced the frustration of being with children who believe that they can have and do whatever they want--to the fatigue and consternation of the rest of us. It seems to me that our sexual "freedoms" are indicators that we are entering the age of lawlessness and godlessness.

> But understand this, that in the last days there will come times of difficulty. For people will be lovers of self, lovers of money, proud, arrogant, abusive, disobedient to their parents, ungrateful, unholy, heartless, unappeasable,

slanderous, without self-control, brutal, not loving
good, treacherous, reckless, swollen with conceit, lovers of
pleasure rather than lovers of God, having the appearance
of godliness, but denying its power. Avoid such people. For
among them are those who creep into households and
capture weak women, burdened with sins and led astray
by various passions, always learning and never able
to arrive at a knowledge of the truth. (2 Tim. 3:1-7)

We have heard over and over that our Western culture is not
healthy. We are overstressed. Overworked. Not enough sleep. We
consume too much alcohol. We are too attached to media and
technology. We are obese. We are sedentary. We are dumbed
down.

Into the pressure of all of this come our children, who now bear
the responsibility to determine if they are male or female, who or
what attracts them and what they want to do about it. The longing
for affirmation, to be known as unique and special, not to be
labelled or put into a group, gets channeled into more and more
bizarre explorations of identity and desire. What an incredible
burden for children to have to carry. The consequences of such
burdens of choice are unknown to us all.

Perhaps in response to this, the Church has had her pendulum
swings. T. S. Sellers documents well the harm of the recent "purity
ring era" that contributed to sexual illiteracy, body shame, guilt of
desire and sexual dysfunction.[1]

In the evangelical world, it is not an easy journey for a woman with
leadership and or preaching/teaching gifts. Historically, we have
been silenced or channeled into lesser roles with lesser titles. Our
ideas and feelings have been minimized or claimed by others. Our
frustration has been seen as inappropriate anger and our
assertiveness as aggression. Sometimes they have been all of
these, but there has been a kind of misogyny that has trickled
down and found expression in the church.

These attitudes have invaded our sexuality. As one recently divorced pastor's wife said,

> My experience of the teaching of sex in the church has been focused on men: the idea that men need sex and want sex more than their wives, that it's a physiological need and that the focus tends to be on men's pleasure and the wife's role to submit and satisfy. I think that typically women also want to have sex and experience pleasure, but that there is little teaching about mutual pleasure. And, little teaching for women about being comfortable in their bodies and with their sexuality.... We are prudes or we are sluts. I'm not sure the Christian culture of purity rings and balls is a good thing.... My gut tells me they lead more to double lives: girls experimenting secretly and not talking about it to keep the good girl image rather than having healthy conversations.

In the swing against radical feminism, many men have been driven into a kind of bifurcation. They may become passive and withdraw from relating, ashamed of their heritage of abuse or misuse of power over women, choosing isolation over the fray of intimacy.[2] Alternatively, they may become more entrenched in a hierarchical and controlling polarization with women. These are not easy days for a man to walk in integrity. If we can identify misogyny in our culture and our church, so we can find misandry. How far we have strayed from the wonderful freedom of Gal. 3:28, "There is neither Jew nor Gentile, neither slave nor free, nor is there male and female, for you are all one in Christ Jesus."

According to Scripture, we are called to be transformed by the renewing of our minds (Rom. 12:1-2). God judges all cultures, affirming that which is good and convicting as sin and idolatry that which is wrong. To serve Him well as Christian leaders in the area of sexuality, we need to do cultural exegesis. This will increase our awareness of how we have been tainted by our own culture.

Reflection: *How has your age affected the way our culture and the Church impacted your sexuality? Do you resonate with Sellers' view of conservative Christianity as causing religious shame and toxicity around sexuality? What historical changes have you lived through regarding views on sexuality?*

Chapter 8: Cultural exegesis

Most of us have heard of biblical exegesis. We turn to Scripture to understand it as close to the original meaning as possible. We draw out or study the subject from within. We seek to understand what the author was saying in historical context, within that book, and in other writings and all of Scripture.

Hermeneutics is applying that derived-from-inside information to our outside, unique context. Eisegesis is when we read into what is in a verse or passage without considering the context.

But what does all of this have to do with culture? By cultural exegesis, I mean a careful study of our culture to understand it and thus to understand how our subject of sexuality relates to it. Wunderink explains in "Reading the World,"[1] that we live in a postmodern, post-Christian and complicated culture:

> The big idea is that we're Christians trying to live the Christian life in the world. But in order to live a Christian life, we have to somehow embody the Word in a world that the Scriptures never envisaged.... We've also got to understand our world.... Cultural exegesis treats culture like a text.... There will be things we can affirm in culture, there will be things we'll have to reject in culture. But to the extent that culture is the product of human beings who bear God's image, there is the possibility that we'll see something of God's image reflected in culture. This is why...we need to do exegesis. We need to find out what's being said and what it means before we can say *yes* or *no* to it.... We need to start asking a barrage of questions.

Missionaries are trained to do cultural exegesis, to go into a different culture and intentionally observe it. Cultural exegesis means discovering why people do what they do as understood from the inside.

According to missiologist Ernest Goodman, we engage in cultural exegesis in three ways: "By immersion in the culture, by personal engagement through relationship with people in the culture who serve as informants and guides, and by dependence on the Holy Spirit."[2]

If we want to learn about how our culture understands sexuality, we must engage with it. Being in the world, but not of the world (John 17:14-16). We cannot do this from a position of negative presuppositions, distance, or fear of contamination. We need to observe, read, and listen--even while we continually ask the Holy Spirit to guide us into all truth and depend on God to deliver us from evil. We remember the way that our Master walked and the company He loved to keep, and we learn to walk with Him.[3]

There is danger with immersion and personal engagement, of course. We all could tell stories of people we know who have had "moral failure" because of their engagement. But without knowing and caring about those who believe and feel differently than we, our adherence to biblical guidelines is superficial and not sacrificial. Goodman adds that,

> The Holy Spirit is our only defense against the charms and temptations that can snare us in culture. Only by walking in total and step-by-step dependence on Him will we learn a culture well enough to be able to engage in missional translation of the gospel into culture.

I would add that we need to be part of a close community that is able to speak into any areas of self-deception that can develop in our inquiry.

In order to understand the rapid changes in Western sexuality, it is helpful to review recent history. Traditionally, the historical church viewed abortion, premarital and extramarital sex and homosexuality as sin. Gender was not separated from birth sex. Marriage was uniquely heterosexual. Monogamy was valued. Infertility was accepted. Christians today are challenged to look at these and many other issues quite differently.

As Christian leaders, we are often bewildered in how to respond to rapid changes, questions and demands. We are silenced by our fears: fears of being called intolerant, of misunderstanding or misinterpreting Scripture, of judging wrongly, of being party to wrong counsel, or of being rejected.

We stand against injustice and oppression. We often do not know how to live out our lives in the footsteps of our Lord, who perfectly embodied grace and truth. We are dismayed by the multiplicity of strongly held yet divergent views about what is right and good-- what Scripture says and how to interpret it faithfully in our context. There is a long continuum of Christian interpretation of Scripture as literal or as metaphorical, from seeing current sexual trends as sinful to a belief that anything in love is permissible. One side emphasizes truth, the other grace. We awkwardly try to find our place strewn across the continuum.

It is important to acknowledge that the authority of the Church and Scripture has been applied to people in a way that is perceived as oppressive. For many, historical and cultural changes mark liberation from oppressive powers. We need to understand that the need to be accepted and to belong are profoundly anchored in us as humans and that the Church has excluded or marginalized those who have been different or viewed as wrong theologically or behaviorally. We need to understand that people with sexual confusion, temptations and failures are desperate to reconcile their lives. Often, we have failed them by trying to change them first. None of us can answer the Lord's call to "Come" and to "Follow Me" already perfected. We come to Him as broken sinners and He accepts us, forgives us, redeems us and changes us.[4] Too often, we have focused on the sexual failures of others even as we have hidden our own.

I have identified three factors that contribute to our rapidly changing culture:

1. Secularization: Although we bear a Judeo-Christian heritage, our Western culture is increasingly secularized. We are post-modern in the sense that we no longer hold to science and technology for our sources of expertise. We are embedded in an existential or essentialist philosophy of being and doing in which we individually determine what is important and true and at any given time. This has profoundly affected our view of Scripture and its authority as a guide for life, belief and behavior.

2. Sexualization: Our culture is increasingly overtly sexual, and explicit sexual material is normalized through marketing and entertainment. Women and children are often victimized. Despite the feminist movement and women's liberation, pornography is easily accessible to most people. Most of us would agree that children are victims in child pornography, but our media tends to romanticize prostitution and porn of "consenting" adults, as if there are no victims.

    Children are knowledgeable about and engaged in sexual thinking, talk and behaviors at ever younger ages. They are exposed to sexual orientation and gender choices in grade school. Pornography is available to child and adult alike.

3. Individuation: We know that we are individualistic in the West. We have been proud of this; we pulled ourselves up by our bootstraps. We made up the motivational line, "God helps those who help themselves" and claim it as Scripture. We have forsaken the benefits and the

profound basis and need for community. We are ill-prepared for marriage and family because we have lived alone, or as if we are alone. We are single, but painfully isolated and lonely.

These cultural forces of secularization, sexualization and individuation put enormous pressure on us. Our sexuality must be actualized in behavior that feels good and makes sense to me and my situation. We reap the consequences in emptiness, addiction, deadness and severe violence to our own souls.

As leaders, we must speak prophetically into the chaos of our world and the haunting chasm in people's souls. If we do not anchor ourselves in God's revealed truth, that plumb line that will hold us to the biblical center of truth, we will rush along with the stream of conformity that leads to destruction.[5]

Reflection: *Can you identify how secularization, sexualization and individuation have affected you, your family and your church? How have your understanding and experience of sex been tainted by these forces? Where are you on the continuum of Scriptural interpretation and cultural exegesis? How has the Church helped or hurt your sexuality?*

Chapter 9: The 3-lens approach for cultural navigation

One of the most painful parts of our current climate is our inability to talk with each other with dignity and respect[1] and to engage in civil discourse about our ideas and beliefs. I remember hearing Os Guinness speak at our church years ago. He spoke passionately about the "closing of the American mind"[2] and our urgent need to attend to the vast changes that were narrowing our worldview and freedom.

Mark Yarhouse, psychologist and Christian sexuality and gender expert, helps us develop cultural exegesis tools around sexuality. He has developed a three-lens approach that enables us to understand our own preconceived notions and how to "navigate the terrain" of sexuality that is fraught with differences, prejudices, misunderstandings and pain.[3] His three-lens approach enables us to communicate with each other across the divides.

1. Integrity: God chose to create humankind in the image of God as male and female. Male and female unite together in an integrated whole that is very good. Monogamous heterosexual lifetime marriage is God's ideal plan. Any change of this creation order and mandate mars God's intent and purpose. Our gendered creation is God ordained; any perceived dissonance between it and our sense of self is submitted to God and the slow process of sanctification. Our sexual desires and sexual orientation and identity are brought under the Lordship of Christ.[4]

2. Disability: All of life and all of creation have been affected by the fall.[5] Our bodies, our desires and our environment

are all flawed and not necessarily by any direct moral action. Yarhouse notes,

> Those who use this lens seek to learn as much as they can from two key sources: special revelation (scriptural teachings on sex and gender) and general revelation (research on causes, prevention, and intervention, as well the lives of persons navigating gender dysphoria).[6]

This lens enables us to see that we all are broken. We view each other with compassion and acceptance. None of us are who we were created to be. All of us know sexual brokenness in various ways.

3. Diversity: The diversity lens understands that the way that a person is—how they experience themselves, their desires, longings and orientation—is to be discovered, celebrated, honored and revered. To go against this personhood is to go against who God has uniquely created that person to be. Yarhouse observes that this lens answers questions about identity—"'Who am I?'—and community—'Of which community am I a part?' It answers the desire for persons... to be accepted and to find purpose in their lives."[7] The diversity lens of celebration counteracts the experience of self or desires as wrong and provides a community of welcome and acceptance that is all too often lacking in the church.[8]

Yarhouse encourages us to listen well to those whose sexuality, choices, behavior and/or identity differ from our own. His three lenses give us a vocabulary and language to "navigate the terrain" of sexuality—to define our own position and those different from us so that we can engage in civil discourse.

In the next section, we will explore a biblical theology of sexuality—how we understand sexuality through the lens of Scripture.

Reflection: *Have your own views around sexuality changed over the past 10 years? How has your church navigated cultural shifts? With which lens are you most comfortable? How will this help you to communicate with others.*

Part Three: Developing a relevant biblical theology of sexuality

There are three things which are too wonderful for me, four which I do not understand; the way of an eagle in the sky, the way of a serpent on a rock, the way of a ship in the middle of the sea, and the way of a man with a maid. (Proverbs 30:19)

In our post-modern world, no story has more validity than any other. "That is your truth; it is not mine." The greatest crime or vice philosophically is to believe that there is absolute truth. When we talk about sexuality through the lens of Scripture, many problems emerge. First, is it possible that there is absolute, universal truth? If so, how can we know it? If God has self-revealed through Scripture, then why are there so many interpretations and how do we know what methodology or hermeneutic to apply to our own culture? What is culture-bound and what applies to us today, and how do we know? What is normative and unchanging, and what is situational? Does dignity and respect require affirmation of differing views? What is the relationship between our call to obey and our call to love and accept? How do we traverse the tension between authority and interpretation without losing the foundational anchor of the Word of God?

Chapter 10: Sex and the Bible

Donald and his wife were virgins when they married. They assumed that this ensured a good sexual relationship. He describes:

> It was like we believed that sealed it. I guess the best word is just "bewildering." We had a terrible honeymoon and were unable to consummate our marriage. When we did, it was painful for my wife. She got scared and the more scared she was, the worse the experience was for her. I felt so guilty about my needs and desires for her! It's taken a lot of counseling and time to straighten it all out for us. We didn't know where to turn—who we could talk to and we really didn't know how to even talk to each other about what was going on. We thought we were the only ones.

I want to address biblical sexuality using Christopher Wright's metanarrative understanding of Scripture.[1] A metanarrative is the "Big Story" of what God is doing across history through and for all people. It is broken into four chapters: Creation, Fall, Redemption and Restoration (although different theologians and authors will use different words to title the chapters). For example, Dr. David Seemuth, New Testament scholar and teacher, proposes a five-chapter gospel: Creation, Fall, Rescue, Wilderness and Restoration.[2]

Whelchel says that

> It is the only story that explains the way things were (Creation), the way things are (Fall), the way things could be (Redemption) and the way things will be (Restoration). The biblical metanarrative makes a comprehensive claim

on all humanity, calling each one of us to find our place in his story.[3]

As Christian leaders, we need a theological basis to enable engagement with a vast array of sexual ethics and to provide basic guidelines for doctrine and behavior both within the church and within society. The need for a clear voice from the church on these matters is critical, both for the health of our own community and for our faithful witness in the world.

Sexuality is a gift of goodness from God to be celebrated. As followers of Jesus, our primary identity is found in Christ and is characterized by trust and obedience to God's will in all areas of our lives, including our sexuality.

As leaders representing the historical conservative orthodox Church, we believe that God's revealed will for our lives is found in Scripture, the inspired, inerrant communication of God (2 Tim. 3:16). Not all questions of life, ethics and behavior are clearly or directly addressed in Scripture. The international, multi-denominational church of Jesus Christ in all her expressions holds different views in areas of doctrine and behavior about sexuality.

My position and filter is a conservative one, based on the "Big Story" of God's work in the world through creation, fall, redemption, and restoration.[4] We live in this period of history as redeemed people, experiencing the Kingdom of God here and now, but not completely and not completely restored as we one day will be. This has huge ramifications for our sexuality.

Reflection: *Have you studied Scripture to understand sexuality? Has it been a part of your teaching and preaching ministry? How would you summarize what Scripture says about sex?*

Chapter 11: Creation

God has created us sexual, gendered beings (Gen. 1:27-28, 2:22) and calls this good—the crowning work of His creation. Together, male and female, we reflect God's image and are of immeasurable worth and dignity. God's design is an inseparable unity of biological natal sex and gender.[1] Each person is known by God and knit together in the womb with intentional design (Ps. 139:16; Jer. 1:5). The human body is the temple of the Holy Spirit and we are to glorify God in and through it (1 Cor. 6:18-20).

Together as image-bearers, men and women were created to be co-regents with God over all of creation. We have unity and freedom (Gal. 3:28) even as we have diversified roles as part of His plan (i.e. mothers/sisters/daughters/wives/fathers/sons/brothers/husbands, prophets and prophetesses, teachers, judges, kings and queens, heads of churches, etc.).

Singleness is an honorable state, affirmed in Scripture. Singleness offers people the opportunity for greater focus on the Lord in time and efforts, while also participating in meaningful, life-giving relationships with others (1 Cor. 7:7-8, 32-35). Singleness is a gift from God to be used for God and His people. All of us experience seasons of singleness and some of us are called to lifelong singleness (Mt. 19:11-12). Christian singleness should be marked by intentional celibacy and abstaining from sexual relationships. Married or single, we are made complete in God through Christ (Col. 2:20).

The God-ordained context for virtuous sexual expression and procreation is marriage, a sacred covenant between one man and one woman (Gen. 2:24; Mt. 19:4-6). The sanctity of the marital covenant is further reinforced by the Old Testament use of the marriage metaphor for intimacy with God and His covenant relationship with Israel. Spiritual unfaithfulness is pictured by metaphors of adultery and prostitution (Ezek. 16:8; Hos. 2:14-20). The New Testament uses marriage, the one-flesh union, as a metaphor of the relationship between Christ and the Church in both the present and in the anticipated new creation of heaven and earth (Rom. 7:1-6; 1 Cor. 6:17; Eph. 5:21-33; Rev. 21-22).

In Scripture, marriage between a man and a woman is a signpost to all of God's redemptive work in creation. Marriage uniquely reflects God's holy character and the interdependent community that eternally exists within the Trinity through the uniting of a man and a woman into "one flesh."

God reserves sexual intimacy for marriage--an interdependent, exclusive, and lifelong commitment between a man and a woman (Gen. 1:27-28, 2:18; Ex. 20:14; Mt. 19:4-6; Mark 10:5-9; 1 Cor. 6:13-20).[2] In every other relational circumstance or stage of life, God's call is to remain celibate (Mt. 19:12; 1 Cor. 7:7-8; 1 Thess. 4:3-8). Genital sexual activity within the faithful marriage commitment is a unifying, relational, wholistic act that mirrors God's own oneness and is a means for us to participate in God's redemptive purposes. Marriage is meant to be the safe place for procreation and profound intimacy ("naked and unashamed") and has implications for our stewardship over creation (Gen. 1:26, 28, 2:24). Marital sexuality requires careful stewardship; it is meant to be celebrated and enjoyed (Pr. 5:18-19; 1 Cor. 6:15-20, 7:3-5)

Chapter 12: Fall

All creation, including our human existence and sexuality, has been damaged by the fall (Gen. 3; Rom. 1:18-32, 3:23, 5:12). We live in a fallen and broken world where the order of creation is no longer intact. Evil confuses, distorts and alienates us from God, causing grief and disappointment (Rom. 7:21-24; Col. 1:21). Sin's impact is seen in our genetics, biology, development, family and cultural environments and personal choices.

Self-perception of sexual identity and gender can vary, change, be fluid and may be influenced by cultural, psychological or biological factors (Mt 19:11-12; Eph 4:17-18).

Scripture shows that sin's impact goes beyond any individual's choice or behavior, touching the community and even future generations (e.g., the sin of Achan and the defeat at Ai in Josh. 7).

Temptation is not sin. Inclinations and desires are not sin. Sin occurs when we yield to temptation, whether in physical action or by dwelling on thoughts of acting upon the temptation. Jesus himself was tempted, yet without sin (Mt. 4:1-11; Heb. 4:15). He calls us and enables us to demonstrate self-control, even in our thought life and emotions (Mt. 5:17-48).

All extramarital genital sexual activity is sin. We are called to flee sexual immorality and honor God with our bodies (1 Thess. 4:3). Jesus makes clear that it is not just our behavior, but our thought-life as well that needs to be trained in purity (Mt. 5:27-28; 2 Cor. 10:5; 1 Tim. 1:9-11). Behavior that is incompatible with God's design for sexual intimacy does not lead to the ideal life for any individual or community.

Historically, the Church developed negative views about sexuality and sexual expression. Sexual sin has been weighted unjustly and leaders have behaved hypocritically. Vilifying, bullying and rejection of fellow image-bearers has been tolerated. We have not taught clearly nor often enough about biblical sexuality throughout the stages of human development. We have not been a safe and welcoming place for those who are struggling, nor provided them with support and resources. We have not provided appropriate guidance and paths of restoration. We, as leaders, must repent of these wrongs and commit to affirm the dignity of every human being (Gal. 6:1-2).

Chapter 13: Redemption

In response to the fall of man and sin's impact upon this world, God sent Jesus, fully God and fully man, to live, die and be resurrected to redeem and restore His creation (1 Cor. 15:20-22; Eph. 1:7; Heb. 9:12). Through faith in Christ, expressed clearly in confession and repentance, we are forgiven and washed clean (Eph. 2:1-10). We are made new creations in Christ and are continually being transformed into His image (Rom. 3:24-26; 1 Cor. 6:11; 2 Cor. 3:18, 5:17; Gal. 2:20; Titus 3:5). Our lifestyle becomes transformed by the rhythm of the Cross: confession, repentance, receiving forgiveness, and receiving comfort for our wounds (Is. 53:5; 1 Pt. 2:21-25). We learn to abide in Christ, and to walk by the Holy Spirit's direction, guidance, and empowering (John 15:4; 2 Cor. 9:8; Gal. 5:21-26).

God's remedy to sin's deception restores our God-intended sexuality, allowing us to steward it in pursuing holiness and communion with Him. No sin is beyond the loving hand of God who offers everyone restoration through Christ Jesus (Rom. 8:35-39).

Obedience is essential to the life of faith (John 14:23-24; James 2:20-24). The process of sanctification, of being made more like our Lord, is often costly and painful (Heb. 12:11), and involves mortification of our sinful desires, our flesh (Rom. 8:5-7, 13; Gal. 5:17; Col. 3:5). Our example is the life and Cross of Christ (1 Pt. 2:18-22).

Life without genital sexual expression is neither deprived nor incomplete (e.g., the life of Jesus, the apostle Paul and the widow Anna). As God's creatures and with God's help, we are to control our bodies and our desires (1 Cor. 9:26-27; 1 Thess. 4:3-5).

Part of our development and sanctification as Christ-followers is to reconcile our sexual identity, gender identity and sexual activity to God's design and will. As Seemuth noted in his five-part gospel, we live in the land in-between, a place of wilderness, awaiting the Lord's return and our full and final restoration. Our sexuality is a holy longing that points to that consummation.[1] As we behold Him, we become more like Him (2 Cor. 3:18; 1 John 3:2-3).

Christ established the church to be a community where redemption can be lived out. Marva Dawn describes social sexuality and how our fellowship together as believers helps to transform and fulfill genital longings that are exacerbated by loneliness and isolation.[2] Sexual integrity and holiness are a journey for every believer and a normal part of Christian discipleship. Jesus is our model; He did not condemn but called for repentance with great mercy and grace towards the most undeserving (John 8:1-11; Eph. 4:32; Col. 3:13; James 3:17.

Chapter 14: Restoration

All of creation is awaiting full freedom from bondage and suffering, groaning for full restoration (Rom. 8:18-25).

At the resurrection, there will be some similarity between our current and resurrected bodies. Jesus tells us there will be no marriage in heaven, but we will be like angels (Mt. 22:23-30). Paul tells us that we will be clothed in imperishable bodies (1 Cor. 15:42-53). This hints at the mystery the new creation holds.

Our purpose to worship and glorify our Lord will be fulfilled, and we will experience the culmination of this life's journey and walk of discipleship (Is. 65:17; Mt. 25:31-40; 2 Pt. 3:13). All things will be made new (Is. 65:17; Acts 3:19-21; Rev. 21:1-5). We will experience true peace, know God's intention for our wholeness, and receive an inheritance that is imperishable, undefiled and unfading (1 Pt. 1:4).

When we see Christ face to face, all that we have sacrificed, experienced or lost in this life due to our journey of discipleship will make sense and be more than worth it (Mt. 19:27-30; 2 Cor. 4:17; 1 Pt. 5:10).

In a time when we are encouraged to live out our felt sexuality and gender and to actualize our changing feelings and desires, a biblical theology of sexuality is a challenging stark contrast. I am unable to answer the important questions of authority and interpretation in a way that will please everyone. From my own lens, I continue to uphold a more literal interpretation of Scripture because of the affirmation of creation themes across the whole canon. Each of us and our churches and organizations will need to enter this fray if we are to stay true to the tenets of our faith with a deep sense of concern and compassion for the ways of this world.

Part Three has addressed God's intention for our sexuality and gender from a conservative perspective. We are created male and female, reflecting His image together. Our sexuality and heterosexual monogamous union and intimacy in marriage is good and reflects God's intimate relation with His people. The fall has affected all of life and perhaps most powerfully in these days, our sexuality. Our Lord's life, death and resurrection bring us redemption and lead us in sanctification. The Kingdom of God is here, but not fully. Today we live "reckoning" all these things to be true and we fight the fight of faith by His power in us. We turn our longings to Him, we take our wounds and failures to Him, and we teach and model this to those we lead. In the next chapter, we will look at our own fallen and redeemed sexuality.

Reflection: *How has your understanding of God's "Big Story" in the history of our humanity affected your understanding of sexuality? How do you bridge cultural exegesis and biblical theology—for yourself and for your church? How do you understand and have dignified discourse with those whose positions are different than yours? How often do you preach and teach about sexuality from a biblical perspective? Do you offer children and youth sexuality classes? Singles' and marital sexuality classes? What changes need to be made to teach biblical sexuality amidst other very loud competing paradigms?*

Part One described the unique challenges that Christian leaders face. Part Two provided a historical cultural review. Part Three developed a biblical theology of sexuality. Now we turn to personal healing.

Part Four: Sexuality and healing within

"Ponder the path of your feet; then all your ways will be sure."
(Pr. 4:26)

Since the fall, nothing is as it should be. That certainly includes our sexuality. From our genetic heredity to our cultural context, from our personal perceptions, desires and proclivities to the unique makeup of those around us, we are not as we were created to be. Part of sanctification is the process of being restored to our creation intent, when all was as it should be, and to grow in the grounding reality of who we are in Christ.

Chapter 15: Your past and sexual history

"No, my brother, do not violate me, for such a thing is not done in Israel; do not do this outrageous thing. As for me, where could I carry my shame? And as for you, you would be as one of the outrageous fools in Israel. Now therefore, please speak to the king, for he will not withhold me from you." But he would not listen to her, and being stronger than she, he violated her and lay with her.

Then Amnon hated her with very great hatred, so that the hatred with which he hated her was greater than the love with which he had loved her. And Amnon said to her, "Get up! Go!" But she said to him, "No, my brother, for this wrong in sending me away is greater than the other that you did to me." But he would not listen to her. (1 Sam. 13:12-16)

Each of us has a unique sexual history that impacts who we are. I recommend that you consider working through your own sexual history. This will help prevent you from being blindsided by needs, desires and temptations. In my work with the homeless or veterans or in my private practice, I asked my patients very personal questions about their sexuality. After an opening explanation, I asked them about their gender, orientation, sexual behavior, number and kind of sexual partners, areas of concern and degree of satisfaction with their sexual life. This confidential assessment was part of a longer health history to enable me to assess health risks, to guide my patients to resources and to provide them with appropriate healthcare and guidance. Ironically, I find that many Christian leaders do not know or understand their own sexual history nor have access to needed education and resources.

I recommend that each Christian leader utilize the following template to journal their sexual history. This then can be shared with a trusted mentor, spiritual director or counselor to determine areas of needed growth and change. This history is one of many that can be found online and was utilized in a graduate course that I co-taught.[1] It is not exhaustive but will help to open areas of discussion for prayer, confession, and a healing growth process. You (and your spouse, if married) will be able to talk more freely about your needs and desires for intimacy as you understand yourselves and each other better.

I know that some of you will have difficulty doing this. Your sexual history belongs to the old that has passed away—all has become new with your salvation (2 Cor. 5:17). You are hesitant to bring up the old; it is under the blood of Christ. All of that is true, but your past is not erased. God wants to bring you healing and wholeness. He will use all of it for His glory and for the healing of the nations. Your interpersonal relating and communion with God may be limited or even darkened due to the unexamined sexual wounds and sin. According to twelve-step wisdom, the locked dogs in the basement can still make a lot of noise.

Start your history with a simple prayer. "Lord, reveal to me anything that has adversely affected me as a sexual person. Thank You that You are with me, and that You love me and counsel me." Set aside several hours to work through this in an uninterrupted and safe environment. Write as fully as you can in each area.

Sexual History

1. Family Attitudes about Sexuality

    a. How open were your parents to talking about sexuality?
    b. What was your experience in asking your parents sexual questions?
    c. What was your knowledge about your parents' sexual relationship?

     d. What advice or prohibitions were you given about sexual
         purity?

     e. Was your opposite sex parent affectionate? If so, how?

     f. How did your same sex parent model their gender and
         masculine and feminine traits?

     g. How did children get attention and affection in your
         family?

2. Early Sexual Experiences

     a. What was your first exposure to the naked body? How did
         you respond?

     b. How young were you when you first explored your own
         sexuality?

     c. Were there any sexual games that you played with other
         children?

     d. What is your first and most powerful early memory of
         sexuality?

     e. Was there any sexual abuse present in your upbringing?
         What impact has that had on you?

3. Childhood Thinking About Sexuality

     a. What were your childhood theories or myths about
         sexuality, conception and birth?

     b. What impact did your peers have on your sexual
         understanding?

4. Adolescence

     a. (Females) How were you taught and prepared for puberty
         and menstruation? Have you conceived outside of
         marriage? Have you had an abortion?

     b. (Males) How were you taught and prepared for puberty,
         nocturnal emissions and how to handle erections
         in public places?

5. Sexual experiences

   a. What was the context of your first climax? What did you think and feel?
   b. Did your view of God and the teachings of the Bible impact your thinking/feeling? How?
   c. If you have practiced masturbation, what emotional, relational or spiritual impact has it had on you?
   d. Has pressure to have a climax caused guilt, shame or control in your marital relationship?

6. Sexuality and Identity

   a. How strong was your identification with your gender as a child?
   b. Were your behaviors, thoughts, mannerisms typical of your gender?
   c. To what extent have you struggled with your birth gender?
   d. Were people attracted to you physically because of your gender?
   e. What was the content of your sexual dreams and fantasies?
   f. To what extent have you experienced same sex attraction, or wondered if you were a homosexual?
   g. Describe the physical/sexual aspect of your dating life.
   h. Has anyone close to you used sexuality to avoid facing painful issues? How has that affected you?

7. Singleness

   a. Have you found ways to address your sexual needs while abiding by God's standards?
   b. Have you been able to work closely with the opposite sex and have non-erotic friendships?
   c. Have you had to deal with unwanted sexual advances of others? How have you handled it?

d. Have you struggled with any guilt from past sexual relationships?

8. Engagement and Marriage

   a. To what extent were you physical or sexual during your engagement time?
   b. How successful were the sexual relations on your honeymoon?
   c. How has the sexual satisfaction, frequency and playfulness changed during your marriage?
   d. How considerate is your spouse in sexual relations with you?
   e. Have you developed any fetishes in order to intensify the sexual experience?
   f. Have you used pornography or other practices (sexting, cybersex, escorts, strip clubs, etc.) at any time in your life?
   g. What impact have pornography and other practices had on your sexual satisfaction, expectations or appetites?
   h. Have you engaged in emotional affairs? Have you used romance literature or tv/movies to fill emotional needs? How has this impacted your relationships?

9. Spiritual and Emotional Issues

   a. How have your past sexual knowledge and experiences impacted your sexual identity, appetites and satisfaction today?
   b. How has your sexual history impacted your relationship with God? (i.e. guilt, shame, expectations, forgiveness)
   c. How has your sexual history impacted your understanding of how God relates to His children?
   d. Is there anything in the past or present that may interfere with your living in God's design and enjoying sexuality the way He designed it to be enjoyed?

10. Summary

    a. Are you satisfied with your sexuality or is there something you would like to change?

    b. If there is something you would like to change, how would you plan to do so?

When you have finished this exercise, take time to pray through it. Are there areas to grieve? Have you shared these wounds before with anyone else? Consider sharing them with a trusted friend or counselor. Are there areas of sin and shame that are secret? "You are only as sick as your secrets" means that the dark and undisclosed parts of our history still have power over us. Ask God to help you find a safe person and place for confession.

    Reflection: *How did you feel reading these questions and journaling your responses? Were there any surprises? Perhaps like Hezekiah with his bad letter, you could lay your history out before the Lord in prayer. Take your wounds to Him for healing. Take your sin to Him for forgiveness. But don't do it alone. Shame and sinful behaviors are nourished in isolation and secrecy.*

Chapter 16: Specific areas of concern for you

Are there patterns of behavior that have plagued you, robbed your marriage bed or put you or others at risk? Consider seeking help from a licensed Christian counselor who is bound by confidentiality.[1] Be ruthless with yourself. Childhood sexual abuse may have affected you profoundly. These things take time, effort and courage to address. It is quite easy to prioritize the ministry and minimize your sexual history, but remember that your sexuality is an essential, God-given part of your identity and worthy of your careful attention. Your sexuality is your God-given passion and creativity; to neglect it causes deadening or disordered expressions.

Remember that the enemy of your souls would like to keep you in sexual bondage. There are so many negative influences outside of ourselves. Tending to our interior life helps us to avoid becoming a kind of suicide bomber with hidden internal sins and wounds ready to explode at any time--hurting those dearest to us as well as those within our desired ministry scope while destroying us.

- Sexual abuse recovery

I am sorry for any of you that have experienced sexual abuse and trauma. The scars can be lifelong and can affect not only our self-esteem, but also our relating in same and other-sex relationships. Our ability to be intimate in marriage will be hindered in ways that are not easy to predict. We are fortunate to live in a time when many resources are available. Personal counseling and marital therapy have come a long way in terms of knowing how to deal with sexual trauma recovery. There are many good sites available online, treatment programs and books. There is no reason to suffer in silence, bearing unnecessary burdens of shame. Consider starting with Dan Allender's books.[2] Focus on the Family is an excellent place to go to find other reliable sources of help.[3]

Most of us will need to go beyond reading to personal interaction. There is an axiom that holds true in sexual abuse recovery: we are wounded interpersonally and so we are healed interpersonally. Sometimes mixed gender groups can help greatly in our healing in relationship with the opposite gender. I have been helped by the writing of Wendy Maltz (*The sexual healing journey,* 2001*)* and Diane Langberg (*Counseling survivors of sexual abuse,* 2003). It can be very helpful to develop care teams around those who are on the long journey of recovery as there can be compassion fatigue of friends and families.[4] We need to be patient with ourselves and the long process of healing, and with our loved ones as they journey with us and we with them.

- Guilt and shame over sexual sin

Scripture tells us that sexual sin is uniquely different from other sin.[5] God's ideal plan since creation is celibate singleness and heterosexual monogamous marriage that reflect the Trinity, Christ and the Church, and community and intimacy of the highest order.[6] Sexual sin seems to have a ready link to the demonic (1 Cor. 6:15-20). Our independent lifestyles and addictive tendencies coupled with stubborn unrepentance lead God to give us over to our disordered and wrong desires (Rom. 1:24-32).[7] We become the thing that we've worshipped, to our profound anguish.[8] Perhaps these are reasons why we experience such guilt and shame around sexual sin. Our sexuality is a source of tremendous energy, creativity and generativity. All too often, that is not the way that we know and experience it.

It is important for us to work through our sense of sin to untangle true and false guilt. This will require help. We must not allow old sin to fester into new sin. Sin is "baffling, cunning and powerful," as 12-step groups note. It is not to be trifled with. Remember the wonderful claims of forgiveness and freedom in Scripture found in

1 Cor. 6:9-11. "But such *were* some of you; but you were washed, but you were sanctified, but you were justified in the name of the Lord Jesus Christ and in the Spirit of our God." Guilt is a judicial declaration of wrongdoing; it is also a feeling of our conscience when we have sinned. Shame is quite different; it is a deep internal sense that we didn't just do wrong, we ARE wrong and bad and unforgiveable.[9]

I love the ministry of Living Waters. Together we learn to live out the rhythm of the Cross. We work through our wounds and learn to take them in community to the Cross and to receive Christ's healing. We also learn to speak our sins out loud, to confess them specifically by name, to bind them to the Cross, to renounce them, to receive forgiveness and to be cleansed and blessed in our new freedom. There are always people in every group who have never told another about their sin and guilt. Many of us have never confessed our sin openly nor been instructed in the "normal" Christian life disciplines of how to renounce sin and repent of it. We have not had forgiveness declared to us. It is wonderful to be reminded that part of our restoration involves receiving Christ's death in our place in full payment of our sin and to accept His cleansing flow and new resurrection life.

Leanne Payne[10] has written about the greatest barriers in Christian life growth to be our inability to forgive others, to receive forgiveness and to accept ourselves. It is no mark of holiness to believe that Christ forgave others but can't forgive us because our sin is too big or too bad. Forgiveness plays a huge role in our personal sexual healing. As we begin to understand and receive forgiveness, so we are able to forgive others. We learn to live out the truth of Eph. 4:32, "Be kind to one another, tenderhearted, forgiving one another, as God in Christ forgave you." Forgiveness restores life and joy to our sexuality.

Clearly it is important to take care of this aspect of guilt and shame in our sexuality before we get into positions of leadership. Many ministries are ruined by sexual sin. We have seen too many examples of old stories coming out to ruin lives that are currently lived in holiness. It is a good goal to live without secrets, to walk in integrity where our talk matches our walk and where we are not vulnerable to disclosures about secret sin in our past or present.

God's forgiveness is the anchor of our testimony so that there is nothing that can be discovered about me or you as a leader that has not been openly shared. Integrity calls us to deal with sin quickly and to open up guilt and shame to the light of our Healer, for whom darkness is as light.[11]

We have lost the art of confession in many of our churches; all too often, it is even missing from our pastoral prayers. We no longer have a mourner's bench for grief over our sin, nor time and place to confess our sins. As leaders, we need to model and teach not only that confession is an essential practice of Christian life, but that forgiveness is real and must be received by faith (1 John 1:7-9). These ancient practices are part of normal Christian life and enable us to dismantle the false images and appearance management of ministry.

Reflection: *Has your childhood inhibited or disordered your sexuality? How and what can you do about it? As you consider past sexual sin, have you been able to receive forgiveness and come to a resolution of shame and guilt? Who can you tell your story to? Who needs to know? Who can help you work through guilt and shame? Make a list of your current support network. Do they know the "real" you?*

Chapter 17: Your present life

"Remember this and stand firm, recall it to mind, you transgressors, remember the former things of old; for I am God, and there is no other; I am God, and there is none like me, declaring the end from the beginning and from ancient times things not yet done, saying, 'My counsel shall stand, and I will accomplish all my purpose.'" (Is. 46:8-10)

We commit our <u>regrets</u> to the Lord and trust Him to bring life from the ashes of our sin and failures. We trust in His forgiveness. We accept the consequences of our sins. We refuse our tendency to expect and demand our loved one's forgiveness, understanding, forgetting and trusting us. We remember that expectations tie us to disappointments. We bring God our true sorrow and lament over the past as it comes up, but we do not dwell in it.

We bring Christ our <u>wounds</u> that may be triggered by many inexplicable things and may tempt us to old ways of relating, behaving, and believing. We believe that we are healed by His stripes, that our Lord understands, as He is a man of sorrows, well-acquainted with grief, who empathizes with all our weaknesses (Is. 53:3-5; Heb. 4:15-16). We grieve freely.

We acknowledge our areas of <u>vulnerability and need</u>, and we take practical steps to protect our loved ones, our church and ourselves. These steps will be different but necessary for each of us. They may entail electronic device filters and avoidance of certain places, reading material, media or people. It may mean avoiding physical expressions of affection, email or texting in certain relationships, or being alone with certain people. It may mean counseling, spiritual direction, established routines of exercise, eating and sleeping. It may mean choosing the practices of spiritual disciplines that best address our weaknesses.[1]

We celebrate our sexuality. We practice gratitude for our gender and our current state of singleness or marriage. We believe what we cannot see and hope in it. We remember all the exhortations in Scripture to be strong and courageous, to fear not for He is with us. We commit to the difficult conversations. We present our gendered selves to the Lord, asking for God's help to be good gifts to others by His enabling.

Today we accept whatever state we are in (Phil. 4:11) with contentment. If single, we praise God for the time and energy to pursue His interests (1 Cor. 7:34), even as we learn to be good gifts to the other gender. As married, we strive with God's striving to know the reality of one flesh, the delights of sexual intimacy and the nurturing of family. We communicate and negotiate with our mate about differences in desire and seasons of anhedonia or sexual tension. We don't deprive each other, nor do we demand of each other (1 Cor. 7:5). We commit to building trust and safety, chastity and integrity in our singleness and in our coupleship, believing God for the all the mystery, wildness and exuberance of our sexuality.

We confess sins as they occur to God and each other. We renounce all sinful, idolatrous thinking (2 Cor. 10:5). We live out the fruit of repentance. We forsake bitterness. We receive His forgiveness. We remember His example of loving His disciples to the end, washing the feet of those who would betray Him (John 13; Phil. 2:1-11).

We courageously forsake self-protectiveness and playing the victim role. We forsake control and manipulation. We renounce misogyny and misandry. We choose to believe the best of the other and to consider the other more highly than ourselves.

We commit to <u>ongoing learning</u> to better understand our own sexual needs and those of our mate, if married. We intentionally prepare to offer ourselves "naked and unashamed" to each other. We commit to ongoing discovery as image bearers. We study to give good counsel that is theologically sound and scripturally grounded. We secure resources at our churches and organizations and continually read for personal growth, edification and healing.

We exercise <u>trust</u> in Him as we deal with unmet needs and unwanted desires. We submit ourselves to His lines for us, lines that we say by faith have fallen for us "in pleasant places" (Ps. 16:6). We don't deny that we are sexual with unique gifts and desires and longings. Our Creator knows what we need before we ask it (Mt. 6:8).

We <u>practice forgiveness</u> with each memory or incidence of offense. We refuse superficial peacemaking and as much as possible, we live at peace with everyone, always striving for reconciliation (Rom. 12:18).

We <u>prayerfully strategize</u> for the future, asking God to use our sexual history, our current context and heart's needs to help us plan for next steps.

You are a leader and there are people around you, watching and waiting for your healing so that they can trust God and His church for their own healing.

Reflection: *What is the current state of your sexuality? What are the areas of growth that you want to address? Weaknesses and vulnerabilities? Areas to celebrate? How can you be bold and courageous in Jesus' presence today? It is a good exercise to check your personal, church and organization libraries. How many books do you find about sexuality—about the theology, ethics and behavioral aspects? How many have you read? Do you have a list of resources that you can use to refer to people who* *seek your counsel? Do you have a list of professionals, clinicians, clinics, hospitals and treatment centers for referrals?*

Chapter 18: Your future

One day, with unveiled face no longer obscured by sin and wounding and ignorance, we shall see Him face to face. Now it is dimly, then it will be so clear (2 Cor. 3:18). There will be no marriage in heaven (Mt. 22:30), no sex as we know it today, but we will have the intimacy we all have longed for from the beginning.

As we live into that future reality, we take responsibility for our sexuality today. We determine areas of ignorance or misinformation and set about learning aright. We examine our past wounds, sin and guilt and we make confession with trusted others. We seek help and accountability for besetting sins and addictions. We do not make friends with Naaman the leper. He scorned getting healed in the Jordan because he had far less humiliating and public ways to do it that were familiar to him (2 Kings 5:1-19). Rather, we seek counsel and receive and follow suggestions with humility. We search for mentors, a spiritual director, a therapist, a health care provider, prayer support, support groups—whatever is needed in our journey of sexual wholeness.

As singles, we commit to celibacy in the wholeness of our sexual, gendered selves, believing God's goodness and enabling. As marrieds, we commit to a lifestyle of service and forgiveness. For some of us, this will mean a journey of great cost and sacrifice, trusting God for His sustaining love along the way. Some will continue with same sex attraction, some with gender confusion and dysphoria. Some will live in unsatisfying marriages, face marital breakup or widowhood; some will long with great loneliness to find a mate. Some will deal with deep betrayal. In all these things, it is essential to remember the promises of our Lord, the man of sorrows well-acquainted with grief, who goes before us. It is through Him that we remember that:

> Christ Jesus is He who died, yes, rather who was raised, who is at the right hand of God, who also intercedes for us. Who shall separate us from the love of Christ? Shall tribulation, or distress, or persecution, or famine, or nakedness, or peril, or sword? Just as it is written, "For Thy sake we are being put to death all day long; we were considered as sheep to be slaughtered." But in all these things we overwhelmingly conquer through Him who loved us. For I am convinced that neither death, nor life, nor angels, nor principalities, nor things present, nor things to come, nor powers, nor height, nor depth, nor any other created thing, shall be able to separate us from the love of God, which is in Christ Jesus our Lord. (Rom. 8:34-39)

As Christian leaders, sexuality is a major method of causing a fatal fall. We must not be surprised by the fiery trials that we have in this area (1 Pt. 4:12). Be committed to education of yourself, your family and your congregation or organization. Be ready to confess sin. Be ready to listen to others' pain and eager to forgive their failures. Trust Jesus, who was tempted in all ways as we are, but was without sin, to guide us into all truth and into the paths of righteousness (Heb. 4:15; Pr. 3:5-6). Make no mistake, we will be like fish swimming upstream in our sexualized world (Rom. 12:1). But oh, the joys of ministering truth to wounded and starving souls that will flock to us as we deal with our own sexuality openly, respectfully and joyfully surrendered to the glory of God.

The integration of our present sexuality will involve addressing our past, acknowledging our present context and entrusting God with our future as we respond to Him in obedience. Today we acknowledge our dependence on the Holy Spirit for the process of sanctification and the restoration of our sexuality.

Reflection: *Take time to thank God for your sure and future hope. Ask Him to help you align your plans for today with that future reality. Write down three practical sexuality goals with measurable steps to achieve them.*

In Part Four, we addressed our personal sexual healing as Christian leaders. Our final section will address specific broad areas of need facing us today: singleness, sex education in the church, and dealing with betrayal.

Part Five: Special Issues

"Thus says the LORD, who makes a way in the sea, a path in the mighty waters, who brings forth chariot and horse, army and warrior; they lie down, they cannot rise, they are extinguished, quenched like a wick: 'Remember not the former things, nor consider the things of old. Behold, I am doing a new thing; now it springs forth, do you not perceive it? I will make a way in the wilderness and rivers in the desert.'" (Is. 43:16-19}

A friend of mine recently told me that she thought that there are two main windows of witness to our world today--trauma and sexuality. All too often, these two collide. All around the world, trauma healing training is requested for the church; all around the world. sexuality questions are emerging.

Many issues around sexuality deserve special attention. There are so many questions and concerns that we are tempted to avoid dealing with them. We tend to vacillate between two poles: "Just the truth and nothing but the truth," or a sort of "Just love them and offer grace."

I have chosen to address three issues that, while perhaps not the most pressing, affect the greatest number of people: singleness, children's sex education and dealing with betrayal.

Chapter 19: Singleness

"You make known to me the path of life; in your presence there
is fullness of joy; at your right hand are pleasures forevermore."
(Psalm 16:11)

We all spend parts of our life single. The percentage of singles in the church is increasing. Many singles continue to feel like second class citizens in the church and feel that marriage is portrayed as the ideal way to be.

Approximately 45% of the U.S. population is single and the number is growing.[1] According to U.S. Statistica Research,[2] about 1/3 of American households are single-person led. These numbers have been increasing since the 1960s.

> In general, Americans are not so eager to commit to partners anymore, this trend is also evident in the declining marriage rate; only a fifth of American men and even less of American women consider marriage a life goal nowadays.[3]

In 2019, research showed that 77% of study respondents believed that love could last a lifetime and 69 percent of respondents stated that they think sex between unmarried partners is morally acceptable.[4] Marriage was not the necessary link.

Another report noted that,

> In 1960, 72 percent of adults were married. Among today's growing single population, 63 percent have never been married, 23 percent are divorced, and 13 percent are widowed. Of that staggering single population, the majority of which are living independently of their own accord, 53 percent of singles are women.[5]

This is important demographic information for Christian leaders to know because these trends are reflected in the church. Nic Fridenmaker, Pastor of High School ministries at Eastbrook Church,[6] observed that there are fewer couples in high school students than in the past, less dating and more group affiliation. This doesn't mean that there is less sexual activity, he notes, but rather a kind of "constant amorphous sexual tension."

What does this mean for Christian leaders working with singles in the area of sexuality? First, we need to evaluate our church for biases that exclude singles rather than integrate them. Second, we need to understand that the singles in our church are not a homogenous mass. They will differ in age, ethnicity, gender and state of singleness, i.e. never married, in a relationship, divorced, widowed, or a combination of these. Their degree of involvement and satisfaction with the church will differ, as will their experience of loneliness.

Each "single" designation has many variations. Have they never married because they are called to celibacy or a celibate vocational ministry? Are they are cohabitating rather than marrying? Is it because they cannot find an interested or interesting partner? Perhaps they are wounded by mistrust in the opposite sex or they are same sex oriented. The causes of divorce are as unique as the couple themselves and widowing creates singleness in varying experiences of grief.

It will not work to throw the word "singles" around as if that will cause inclusivity and a sense of belonging. Rather as with most things in our complex world today, we will need to study our people, listen to them and stay current with research.

We may need to address any ways in which we have segmented our community and worship by age or gender. Simple things like providing women's Bible studies during the day might exclude many working single women. Single parents' involvement will necessitate creating safe childcare. Single seniors may need daytime fellowship and transportation help. None of these things can be known unless we look for them and listen to the answers in our assessment.

Sexual attitudes and behavior cannot be assumed given the great diversity of singles. To assume that all singles are sexually abstinent or celibate will alienate a large portion according to statistics, however, assuming that all are or have been sexually active is extraordinarily offensive.

Erica Breitbarth recently shared her story at the conclusion of a five week preaching series on sexuality at her church. She asked, "Why would you have someone who is celibate speak on sexuality?" She then grounded her words, "Guess what? Jesus was single and He is our model for how to live the perfect life!" She provided three examples of negative church experience that can help us.

1. "There's a man out there for you." This unfortunate but well-intentioned statement awkwardly communicates that status and maturity are connected to marriage and that single people are immature, incomplete and needing to be fixed. Breitbarth quoted John Blatther: [7]

> One of the first things we can do to strengthen Christian marriage is to support singlehood. If people are to enter marriage wisely, they need to be free of inordinate pressures to 'escape' the single state. We should view singlehood not as a 'holding pattern' for the immature, but as a viable option for fruitful Christian life and service. The more viable singlehood is in the church, the fewer bad choices will be made about whether, when, and whom to marry.

2. "I know this must be a hard day for you." This was expressed with feeling at both wedding and baby showers. Breitbarth struggled with how to respond. The statement implied that she was longing to be married and longing to have a child, something that may or may not be true for any single. She notes that there is a theologically incorrect assumption involved. Our first family is the Church (Mt.

12:48-49). Single people demonstrate the covenant relationship between Christ and the church.[8] Singleness is a God-affirming, fruitful way of life.

3. The prevalence of abstinence promises and purity pledges: Breitbarth noted that implicit in these movements is a sense of deprivation that will be rewarded and filled in marriage. There is a message that if you remain abstinent, you will find God's mate for you and you will have a wonderful sexual relationship. Not only has this not been an effective method of delaying sexual behavior, but this kind of thinking leads to doctrinal confusion, works righteousness and deep disappointment. She added,

> The issue lies in separating sexuality from intimacy with others. You can live without sex, but you can't live without intimacy. You can also have sex without intimacy, as our culture demonstrates. Oftentimes singleness is modeled as what we can't do rather than what we can do! I'm not abstaining from intimacy--I just serve with my body in a different way. Our bodies are a gift to one another! Single people express their sexuality through connection and love for others around them. This is radical and countercultural, because it is about giving rather than receiving.[9]

Breitbarth understands her singleness through the lens of Is. 54. In it, the prophet Isaiah personifies Jerusalem as a woman without children. In that time, barrenness was a thing of great shame. Having children was a sign of God's favor. Is. 54:1 turns that around, displaying God's goodness, restoration and redefinition of family: "'Sing, O barren one, who did not bear; break forth into singing and cry aloud, you who have not been in labor! For the children of the desolate one will be more than the children of her who is married,' says the Lord." Joy and song are the response and barrenness becomes the ground of fruitfulness.

Verse 2 is a familiar promise, "Enlarge the place of your tent, and let the curtains of your habitations be stretched out; do not hold back; lengthen your cords and strengthen your stakes." Breitbarth sees this enlargement as single Christians pour their lives into the marginalized both inside and outside the church.

She continues with verse 5, "For your Maker is your husband, the LORD of hosts is his name; and the Holy One of Israel is your Redeemer, the God of the whole earth he is called." A single is whole without a spouse because they are deeply and intimately connected with their Creator. She affirms, "My only covenantal relationship on this earth is with God, which provides me more space for contemplation and connection with Him."

She concluded her story with verses 11-12, "O afflicted one, storm-tossed and not comforted, behold, I will set your stones in antimony, and lay your foundations with sapphires. I will make your pinnacles of agate, your gates of carbuncles, and all your wall of precious stones." In these verses, Breitbarth takes comfort that though the world may not understand, God promises that He will honor, celebrate and make beautiful the single person. Though suffering may come, He will affirm and bless.

Liz Carver, Director of Communication at Eastbrook Church, writes that the narrative about singleness in the church is narrow and non-biblical—a kind of shallow, single story, rather than a rich multi-layered story. It is "reinforced through interactions, language, programming, events, imagery, and even Biblical interpretation.... We have created a church in which Jesus Christ would not belong."[10] She continues,

> A theology of singleness has little to do with romantic or sexual singleness and has everything to do with the individual's single-minded, integrated understanding of self in relation to God. Therefore, it is open to every Christian, regardless of age, stage, marital, or dependent status. A theology of singleness is Biblical, is a part of patristic and pre-modern church tradition, and if adopted

once again, would benefit all social relationships within the church, including marriages.

So much of what has been preached and taught about single sexuality revolves around abstinence or responses to "How far can you go?"[11] rather than the rich and full intimacy that is grounded in a theology of the body. As leaders, we must call all the Church to "locate their identity first and foremost in Christ above all other identity markers."[12] This is true for all believers in Christ. As the Apostle Paul wrote, "For you have died, and your life is hidden with Christ in God" (Col. 3:3).

Here are some leadership principles for growing healthy singleness in your congregation.

1. Know your church or organization. Do regular surveys to determine the demographics of your group. Avoid making assumptions about marriage, singleness and/or sexuality.

2. Intentionally connect singles to the greater church body. Incorporate singles and single viewpoints in organizational leadership, teaching and preaching.

3. Include a biblical theology of singleness in your theology of the body. Carver notes,

> A theology of singleness provides space for a healthy practice of celibacy, but it requires that we both debunk the myth that perfect sexual fulfillment occurs within marriage, and also that we debunk the myth that celibacy is a second-class practice. We must regain a high view of celibacy, as it is a practice that we will all exercise, even if only for a season.[13]

4. Affirm celibacy and assist in the development of this discipline through teaching, fellowship and counsel. Celibacy is grounded in the broader life of chastity, a lifestyle of self-giving. Carver notes that

the celibate life requires a reordering of desires in a way that is oriented towards God's priorities rather than our own. A proper theology of singleness must have, at its core, a proper ordering of desires in a way that prioritizes God over personal pleasure.[14]

Reflection: *What has your experience of singleness been like? Have you experienced celibacy as poverty or fruitfulness? How has your identity grown in Christ? Has your church prioritized marriage? How can a theology of singleness enrich your fulfillment as well as that of your church or organization? Take time to pray about your own foundational identity in Christ.*

Chapter 20: Sex education for children and youth

"Whoever receives one such child in my name receives me, but whoever causes one of these little ones who believe in me to sin, it would be better for him to have a great millstone fastened around his neck and to be drowned in the depth of the sea."
(Mt. 18:5-6)

We all long for children to grow up happy, healthy and wise. Their unhappiness breaks our hearts. None of us want to be an obstacle in their path. Instead, we want to make straight their ways and lighten their loads.

I regularly have parents ask me why there is so much more mental illness in children and youth today. Is it because of vaccines? Over-diagnosing and over-medicating for attention deficit, depression and anxiety? Could it be poor diet? Lack of exercise? Too much homework? Exposure to media? Pornography? Broken homes? Bullying? Pace and stress of life? Poverty? Racism? Immigration? Addiction? Climate change? Guns, violence and school shootings? Suicide? Abortion? Risky behaviors? Substance use?

We have reason to be very concerned for our children and their health. Today's hypersexual culture and world view of sex as a pivotal factor of identity and happiness plunge our children into ever greater stress. Now they have the burden of identifying and following their own desires, whatever they are and wherever they may lead.[1] This is a kind of social experiment that we don't have data on. How will a looser family structure affect children? How will genetic engineering affect them? Does the constellation of the family matter (2 mothers, 2 fathers, single parent moms and dads, etc.)? Does it matter if they and/or their parents choose hormonal or surgical gender changes to conform to their sense of self? Does it matter that they can practice "safe" sex with minimal measurable consequences?

All of these are important questions that can be debated, but long-range studies—longitudinal research—are lacking. As Christians, we need to understand these times (1 Chronicles 12:32) and continue the task of raising our children, training them in the way that they should go (Pr. 22:16). But what is that way and how do we do it when it comes to sexuality? Given our cultural context and the pressures placed on even young children to be sexual, it seems clear that education must include sexuality and issues of sex.

Sex education used to be a private thing that took place within the home, but over time that education proved insufficient. As our culture has been urbanized and family size has decreased, children do not have the same opportunities to learn about reproductive function as they did in a rural farming context or in a larger family. The church became involved in sex education and soon the schools became involved. As often happens, sex education has swung on the pendulum of too little, too late to too much, too soon. Today, children are bombarded with sexual content from both media and secular education.

The Catholic Church has reiterated its concern about school sex education and the need for it to be provided primarily in the home. In 1996, The Truth and Meaning of Human Sexuality: Guidelines for Education within the Family (TMHS) was published.[2] This document details the history of the school taking responsibility for sex education from the home. Initially the church and school were "subsidiary" supports to the parents. But over time, and with cultural change, schools became the primary providers of sex education.

Whitehead[3] warns that it is important for parents to know what is being taught in the area of human growth and development, i.e. sexuality, in our schools. Usually there is the opportunity for the parent to have the child opt out of certain lessons. However, it is likely that children will still learn from the other children what is being taught.

In an informal survey of area Christian schools, there was no specific curriculum for sex education. In contrast, I was surprised to find that Wisconsin schools do have curricula and that names of body parts with pictures are being taught. I wonder how many of us would prefer that we teach this in the privacy of our own homes and not in a room of 6-year old boys and girls together? Here are suggestions provided for these teachers:

> Say, "Most of these body parts are the same for everyone. But our bodies are not the same in every way. The body parts on the outside of our body that makes us different are in the area where our urine/pee comes out, the penis and vulva." Say, "These parts are often called our 'private parts.' Private parts include the penis, vulva, anus, chest and breasts. Sometimes when people talk about these parts, they will say, 'the parts covered by your swimming suit.' There is nothing bad about these parts. These parts of your body belong to you, and no one else has the right to touch them or look at them without your permission."[4]

By fourth grade, the teacher can decide to keep boys and girls together or separate them for teaching on puberty with male and female anatomical models. Menstruation, ejaculation and HIV/AIDS education is provided.[5] By seventh grade, there is detailed information about reproduction, sex, sex abuse, sexting and sexually transmitted diseases.[6] There are helpful communication exercises available for the parents on the website and many resources are offered. But clearly, the school is in control of sex education and its content and most parents are not aware of what their children are being taught.

Whitehead provides 4 guidelines for sex education:[7]

1. Human sexuality is a sacred mystery and must be presented according to the doctrinal and moral teaching of the Church, always bearing in mind the effects of original sin.

2. Only information proportionate to each phase of their individual development should be presented to children and young people.

3. No material of an erotic nature should be presented to children or young people of any age, individually or in a group.

4. No one should ever be invited, let alone obliged, to act in any way that could objectively offend against modesty or that could subjectively offend against his or her own delicacy or sense of privacy.

Whitehead expresses the deep concern of the Catholic church that children are being sexualized and eroticized at an early age outside of the guidance and protection of their family. What is being taught and the way that it is being taught is dissociated from its grounding in creation in the image of God and the concomitant values of modesty, purity, chastity and morality.

> The Catholic tradition in this matter is: sexuality has been part of God's plan from the beginning and thus it is very good; sexuality is inextricably related to love and life and to lifelong self-giving, whether in marriage or in celibate chastity; but owing to sin, sexuality can be willfully and grossly misused, and for this reason every human person is called to purity and chastity no matter what his state of life.[8]

I interviewed four area children and youth pastors for their perspective on the issue of sex education in the church. Laure Herlinger[9] said that it is like the kids are out in the ocean, having to swim without any protective barriers in sight. They are confused and insecure. Parents often feel ill-equipped and confused themselves. The church wants to welcome all and yet still uphold moral boundaries, but neither the church nor the parents know how. We need to help parents educate their children and encourage loving those on the margins while still maintaining carefully thought through limits. Parents need time to meet each other and together be able to talk about all the issues facing their children and how to parent them. Sometimes, just providing opportunities for parents to get together and discuss these matters provides them with support and normalization. They are not alone in dealing with difficult issues around sexuality.

A few years ago, Pastor Herlinger wouldn't have wanted to include sex education in Sunday school and she doesn't want to now either. However, with the open acceptance of gay marriage and gender fluidity, parents need support in helping young children navigate these waters. "We need to help parents think proactively." She recommends special parent workshops addressing areas of need and providing resources. Staff need to stay abreast of cultural changes and current resources and be ready and available to support parents and children.

Herlinger noted an interesting phenomenon. Because of their compassion, Christian youth may be more likely to be exposed to those with ways of being that are marginalized. Their parents will need to carefully help them navigate the tricky waters of gender and orientation fluidity. If parents aren't informed, they cannot help their children. Parents need to be ready! They need to uphold a biblical view of marriage and singleness. Marriage is not a "charred work," but good. Children need godly models and good examples of marriage and singleness. They need to see God's good design in how He made us, and how marriage and singleness are pictures of God's love for us.

Leslie Osborne was a pastor of children and family ministry for thirty years.[10] She also expressed concern about the pressure on children to be sexual. She emphasized that the church needs to take an active role in helping parents know how to educate their children—not just in the mechanics of sex, but in a wholistic foundation from birth on of who they are in Christ. Children need to be affirmed and given a healthy sense of self. Parents need to be regularly reminded and assisted in intentional and spontaneous age-appropriate discussions about sexuality.

Osborne and Herlinger noted the increased cultural stereotyping of male and female roles. A girl is no longer just a tomboy but might be gender dysphoric. A boy who is drawn to beauty, music and creativity might be gender confused or gay. What our culture calls freedom seems to be greater role stereotyping. In the church, Osborne noted, we need to model the broad expanse of ways to be male and female. Parents need help in how to talk about homosexuality and transgender because it is "tricky." Part of the role of the church is to help parents to get healthy so they can better nurture their children. Things like stranger awareness, abuse and sex trafficking must be addressed. "The church is failing on this level. Our kids are hearing all sorts of stuff from the culture first and last."

Janis Ryder, Pastor of Ministry to Children and Family,[11] notes the difficulty of providing needed education and parental support in the context of a large busy church on Sunday mornings. She and Herlinger recommend children's midweek, gender-separated clubs.

Ryder emphasized the need for early and ongoing education, "You don't give matches to a 2-year old, but you want your 10-year old to know how to use them correctly." In her growing church, the need for education is recognized, but there is no formal equipping of staff or parents. Unless something comes out in a Sunday School lesson (e.g. Rahab the harlot, or the problem of barrenness), nothing is taught. It is the teacher's prerogative. She wishes that it could be a more "normal part" of what happens.

Pastor Nicolas Fridenmaker[12] underlined the necessity for parental involvement as well. He believes that part of why we are in the difficult position we are today is because parents have abdicated their responsibility for sex education in the home. Both he and Osborne agree with what research has shown: abstinence and purity programs have not been successful. They have not been located in a wholistic theology of the body. They have emphasized abstinence from intercourse over chastity--the self-giving and self-mastery training of sexuality. They have been shame-based.

Fridenmaker notes that the need for sex education is at its greatest today because of the cultural messages and worldview. Unfortunately, there are hidden expectations in the church that are born of ignorance. For example, parents think that the church is talking about sexuality and the church believes that the parents are talking about it. In reality, no one is. Youth are being educated by their peers and their culture.

Fridenmaker believes that youth need to see our mistakes and need to have honest and transparent conversations about sexuality. If we wait until they are 17, it is too late for they are already sexually awakened. They are confused about their attractions, their desires and their gender identity. Staff and parents need to be prepared for the individual and spontaneous conversations that may arise.

Every three years, Fridenmaker provides a theology of the body curriculum for middle and high school students.[13] There is a parent's lesson that goes out each week. He, like Herlinger, wonders if the church isn't giving a subtle message that marriage isn't working. We need to celebrate that marriage is good and singleness is good. Chastity is for all of us.[14]

Cameron Cole notes that we must explain "how sex fits within the broader context of biblical theology. If we don't, we set students up for failure, frustration, and despair."[15] Sexuality is a part of God's plan for intimacy that is fulfilled in relationship with Him. We should offer youth a hopeful, God-centered perspective:

> Your desire for sex really is a desire for deep connection with God and people. You do not have to wait until marriage to experience and enjoy intimacy. It is available for you here and now in your relationship with Christ and through vibrant friendships. Perhaps sex will be one of many ways that you enjoy intimacy at some point in your life. However, sex is only one way. Better options exist before and even after marriage.[16]

Parents must reclaim their responsibility for sex education. They need to know what the church and the school are teaching. They need to be prepared for spontaneous questions about sexuality. They benefit from interactions with other parents and from teaching from the pulpit. They need ongoing education through workshops, seminars and connection with other parents.

Here are some recommendations for Christian leaders as they consider their work with children and youth.

1. Honor the parents' involvement. Include them. Equip them. Guide them. Offer them resources. Remind them and exhort them of their responsibility to educate their children in the home. Encourage them to know what is being taught in the church and the home and to advocate for their child's education and protection.

2. Preach and teach about sex education in the pulpit. The Bible is open about many sexual failures. Take time to discuss and explain them. Plan a yearly message that addresses the theology of the body.

3. Honor and celebrate singleness. Integrate singles at every level of leadership and church life and involve them with children and youth ministries.

4. Honor and celebrate marriage. Provide pre-marital courses and counseling. Provide marital enrichment classes and seminars. Involve married couples in children and youth ministries

5. Equip your staff and volunteers to teach about sexuality and to respond to hot topics. Bring in experts. Send them to trainings. Stay current with research, culture, theology and resources.

6. Provide access to resources for parents and youth. Include resources in your bulletins. Highlight them from the pulpit. Encourage their study in small groups.

7. Pray. Pray for wisdom and discernment and an understanding of the times. Pray for those who are struggling or marginalized and welcome them into your church. Pray for your staff, their marriages and families, their singleness, their sexuality. Pray for your congregants and youth who are under tremendous confusion and temptations. Pray for yourself.

8. Be marked by forgiveness. Be patient and hopeful in restoration. Teach and include in your children and youth groups the practices of confession and forgiveness.

9. Entrust the children and youth of your church to His care and entrust the legacy of the church to their future leadership.

10. Glorify God with your body! Model this and be open and willing about what this means to you.

    Reflection: *How did your church teach you about sex as a child? What does your church do now to assist parents in sex education of their children? Take time to review the resources at the end of this book under "Sex Education." Make a plan to fill in the gaps of your own education. Ask God to prepare and enable you to help the youth in your church or organization grow in a healthy sense of self and sexuality. Pray for the children of your church and their leaders.*

Chapter 21: Betrayal

"You shall not move your neighbor's landmark, which the men of old have set, in the inheritance that you will hold in the land that the Lord your God is giving you to possess."
(Deuteronomy 19:14)

"The most difficult part, the secret, the clandestine nature. I remember saying to my husband that his struggle with pornography didn't scare me as much as his ability to sequester that part of his life and keep it from me and his family so thoroughly, when we thought we knew him and we didn't. That scared me more and it still does. I'm like, God, how am I going to know if I really know him? That's what hurt me the most is that feeling of thinking that I know someone, feeling like I am really close to that person and then obviously I'm not close enough for them to trust me with their deepest struggle." Joy, missionary in South America

As Christian leaders, we will need to care for both the betrayed and the betrayer. All of us know the pain of betrayal and can acknowledge that we, as those who have missed the mark (Rom. 3:23), have betrayed our Lord. We can feel David's pain because we too know what it is like to be betrayed by those close to us. We can join in David's lament,

> For it is not an enemy who taunts me—then I could bear it; it is not an adversary who deals insolently with me—then I could hide from him. But it is you, a man, my equal, my companion, my familiar friend. We used to take sweet counsel together; within God's house we walked in the throng.... My companion stretched out his hand against his friends; he violated his covenant. His speech was smooth as butter, yet war was in his heart; his words were softer

than oil, yet they were drawn swords. (Ps. 55:13-14, 20-21)

The sexually betrayed long for their offender to understand the profound nature of their offense, which at heart, is a sin against God's faithfulness. The offender wants their confession and repentance recognized and for forgiveness to include the reestablishment of full trust.

Sexual betrayal contains a wide continuum of behaviors that can include pornography, sexting, internet sex, strip clubs and escort services. It can include emotional affairs, fantasy and compulsive masturbation. Its contours are ever expanding, and the betrayal is best explained by those experiencing it.

In my doctoral work,[1] I researched the phenomenon of healing in missionary women who had experienced sexual betrayal in their marriage. I conducted extensive interviews and was blessed to bear the weight of their stories, some of which had never been shared before. I discovered certain common themes. The women told me what had helped and what had hindered their healing; they provided recommendations for the church and their mission organizations. What surprised me most in the aftermath of this work was that men shared that these themes and recommendations resonated with their experience of betrayal as well. People that had experienced sexual abuse or domestic violence connected with these themes. Betrayal seemed to unite their differing experiences of pain.

It is not surprising that those sexually betrayed describe it as "shattering." Christians have an expectation of childhood safety, of relational fidelity—especially in marriage--and of integrity in the innermost parts. Unfaithfulness in relationship, sexual sin and abuse are marked by deception and secrecy and often revealed only under duress. The betrayed individual's understanding of their world, their relationship, and the way they believed things were and should be, are all horribly broken.

When I travel internationally to talk about trauma healing, I take 2 hand-held mirrors with me. I ask participants to look in the mirror and to tell me what they see. Depending on the culture, they will look at themselves briefly and report that they see their face. Then I pass around a mirror that has been shattered. Shards of glass are missing, others are in danger of falling out and indeed, the mirror must be held carefully to avoid splintering and injury.

What do they see as they observe themselves? Most do not enjoy looking at themselves in this shattered mirror. Their image is distorted and troubling. I ask, "Can this mirror be repaired? Will it ever return to a perfect reflection?" Even those who think that it can be repaired acknowledge that it will never be the same. Some pieces are missing that cannot be replaced. Even the best of glues cannot pull together the small irregular pieces that have resulted from the breakage.

A person who has experienced sexual betrayal will never be the same. They require God's extraordinary love, grace and restoration. The Christian leader is called into this difficult healing work.

For some, sexual betrayal compounds earlier trauma. In our mirror example, the handle and back of the mirror are intact. What would happen if they also were broken? Some experience the betrayal of sexual sin as life-threatening. Their whole sense of self was already fragile. Perhaps they have a history of childhood sexual abuse, neglect or abandonment. Or perhaps they have known significant betrayal in a previous relationship or were raped. For these, the discovery of unfaithfulness in marriage or church leadership might be like a broken mirror in a broken handle.

In my research, I discovered that the women worked very hard to understand what had happened in their marriage and to determine the causes of betrayal. They chose one or more frameworks to make sense of the chaos of their brokenness. They identified spiritual warfare. Satan, after all, is out to steal, kill and destroy (John 10:10a), running about like a roaring lion seeking to devour them, their family and their ministry (1 Pt. 5:8). Some women noted that their husbands were exposed to a kind of dark seduction because of the unredeemed culture that they lived in. Others noted the temptations now available through the Internet, where powerful desires could be fueled through accessible, affordable and anonymous (the "Triple A") sex.[2] These women tended to sympathize with their husband's vulnerability and feel anger against the evil one and all of his schemes. Their response was prayer, spiritual warfare and deliverance ministries.

Others understood their husband's bondage through the lens of addiction. In this worldview, sexual addiction was seen as a disease with the wife bearing 50% responsibility as the codependent enabling part of the dynamic. These women do not blame their spouse but take responsibility and seek to address their own sickness through 12-step groups such as CoDA, Al-Anon, S-Anon or Celebrate Recovery.

Many women blamed themselves. They were not attractive enough, not sexy enough, not thin enough. These women worked hard to become what their husband liked and were vulnerable to the pull of pornography as they tried to see the world through his eyes. They changed how they dressed, tried to imitate sexual behaviors, or engaged in odd requests from their partner. They objectified other women, analyzing their breasts or genitalia or legs or facial expressions, always wondering, "Is that what he likes?" In so doing, the objectification that is part of sexual addiction extended from husband to wife. Some women found themselves thus being attracted to women as they lived through their husband's eyes.

Some women were able to comfort themselves with the knowledge that it wasn't their fault because their husband had wanted something very different. The women whose husbands struggled with same sex attraction felt that it wasn't that *they* were rejected; it wasn't another woman he wanted; it was a man. Or it was women of a different ethnicity. Or a child. This sense of "other" attraction took the terrible load of guilt off the wife; it wasn't her fault that she wasn't a man, that she wasn't Black or Asian, that she wasn't a child. This perspective enabled them to have compassion on their spouse.

An understanding of trauma helped some to make sense of their responses—the preoccupation and flashbacks, the irritability and hypervigilance, the numbness and negative outlook, the sense of unreality. These women prioritized their own healing from trauma.

Most of those betrayed experienced depths of rage that were unimagined before and even engaged in violence against their mate. They prayed that he would die, or they prayed that God would take them first. Anger became corrosive contempt against the offender. The husband must fully confess and repent. He must turn away completely from whatever constituted his betrayal. When that didn't happen, or when relapses occurred, the betrayed were left raging at God.[3]

Themes of betrayal

1. The betrayed work hard to develop a framework of meaning. The following factors helped the wounded partners to make sense of the chaos.

   - Addiction: The betrayed is equally to blame because they enabled the sin.
   - Spiritual warfare: The betrayer was deceived or influenced by Satan and not personally fully responsible.
   - Idolatry: The offender made their desires an idol, the offended made their partner an idol. Therefore, unfaithfulness was God's severe mercy to break the relational idolatry.
   - Stress: The individual or couple is in a context of great pressure and used sexual sin to medicate that stress.
   - Sexualized culture and context: The offender was weakened by culture and constant temptation.
   - Systemic evil in church or mission: Charming, effective and narcissistic personalities were valued over character so that deception and hypocrisy were not addressed.

2. The way that the betrayal was disclosed profoundly affected the healing process.

- Complete and fast disclosure facilitated healing, recovery and rebuilding of trust.
- Incomplete disclosure over time increased mistrust and reduced the likelihood of marriage reconciliation and restoration.
- Most disclosure was forced, discovered by the spouse or third party and not initiated by the offender.
- The betrayed differed as to the degree of disclosure that they needed or wanted; this was best facilitated in consultation with a mental health professional.

3. The length of recovery is longer, and the process of recovery is deeper than ever desired.

- "True repentance"[4] facilitates healing and recovery.
- Relapses and evidence of ongoing deception make the recovery process far more difficult.
- Becoming involved in ministry to other wounded individuals or couples helps recovery.
- Most need a period of physical and sexual separation to process the situation, to avoid violence and to express the seriousness of the betrayal and broken vows.
- Minimization or denial of the extent and impact of the offense prolongs recovery.
- The process of healing is longer for the offended spouse than for the offender.[5]

4. Strong emotions of grief and anger are part of the healing process.

- Grief is silenced and complicated by the need to protect reputation, to protect children, or because of a lack of safe places to express pain.

- Depression, a sense of paralysis or numbness and physical illness are common companions of grief.
- Symptoms of post-traumatic stress (shock, confusion, numbing, avoidance and hypervigilance) are common. This may include "espionage."[6]
- Unhabitual expressions of violence are possible: hitting partner, throwing and breaking things.
- Suicidal and homicidal thoughts (that God would take them or their mate) are common.
- Many feel silenced by their circumstances and lose their sense of voice and sense of self.
- It is not unusual for women to experience pornography as more difficult than recovery from actual physical affairs.[7]

5. Broken trust is the most painful loss in sexual betrayal.

- For many, the rebuilding of trust is long, even lifelong and trust is never the same.
- Many question their mate's "sobriety" and their own ability to know with certainty if the offender is telling the truth. The betrayed often feel shame about their naiveté—they should have known.
- Many are disturbed by their partner's ability to deceive them repeatedly over time.

6. Recovery from marital sexual betrayal is a lonely process and includes the loss of friends and loss of church.

- The loss of friends is unexpected. Friends drop away because of how long recovery takes, because they believe that the offended party is guilty for not meeting the other's needs and/or because they doubt the reality of the offender's repentance.
- God provides a special sense of His care and love in betrayal through verses, words and visions. However,

most question God's love and care during the disclosure of betrayal.

7. The betrayed person's relationship with the church is significantly altered.
   - The church wants to help but doesn't know how and experiences its own betrayal (especially when unfaithfulness occurred in leadership).
   - The church doesn't know how to exercise discipline; any plan of restoration is usually flawed and not followed. True repentance is difficult to measure.
   - The church may prioritize damage control and protection of the congregation, neglecting the individualized care of the wounded spouse, children and family unit.
   - Many experience the church's failure to care as another betrayal, even more painful and difficult to forgive than the actual sexual betrayal.
   - Many end up changing churches to find welcome, acceptance and care elsewhere.
   - Child molestation, child porn and same sex behavior is considered more sinful and even unforgivable in and by the church.
   - There is often a lack of visitation, calls and practical expressions of concern in the immediate aftermath of revealed unfaithfulness.
   - Anger, particularly female anger, is not handled well and may be shamed by church leadership. Some women live with an oppressive view of submission and headship. Some men live with shame about their masculinity and efficacy.
   - Much of church discipline is administered by men and this can be retraumatizing for women.
   - If the individuals leave the church, there is no ongoing contact or care from the home church, causing a sense of rejection and abandonment.

8. Helpful resources were discovered by the betrayed.

- Resources that are most helpful are about growing closer to the Lord, not about sexual sin.
- The practice of spiritual disciplines is essential (the Word, prayer, fasting, solitude) for survival, grounding and recovery.
- Individual counseling is important, and treatment is essential. Close fellowship of accountability and support groups help to heal.
- There is a strong need for trustworthy, understanding listeners. Older individuals tend to have the least support, counseling and treatment.

Recommendations to Churches and Christian organizations

1. Be prepared for a long process of recovery. Offer initial trauma response with assessment and provision of safety needs. Maintain regular contact by phone, email and visits during the early weeks and months after disclosure. Maintain contact through and after restoration, resignation, or dismissal.

2. If the offender is removed from ministry, look for ways to affirm and continue the ministry of the offended spouse.

3. Help provide healthy closure. Work with the couple to determine ways to explain and say necessary goodbyes to colleagues and church members.

4. Maintain a list of local resources and treatment options. Develop and maintain a collegial relationship with clinicians, i.e. pastoral care specialists, member care providers, spiritual directors, psychiatrists, psychologists, mastered social workers, group therapists, sex therapists and medical providers.

5. Make timely and appropriate referrals. Be prepared for the contradictory needs to protect spouse and children, to repeatedly listen to the story and to provide safe expression of feelings of shock, grief and rage.

6. Be aware of the possibility of domestic violence and suicidality. Assess for these in a matter-of-fact manner and provide monitoring as needed. Refer for treatment as appropriate.

7. Be aware of and assess for the possibility of ongoing and/or recurring deception and marital betrayal. Require and enable accountability. Require computer filters. Encourage and facilitate marriage mentoring. Listen carefully to the spouse's perception of deception. Work with the couple to develop an individual and joint relapse prevention plan.

8. Work towards marital reconciliation and ministry restoration. Refuse to be rushed in the processes of discernment, treatment, accountability and mentoring. After the initial treatment, invite the offending spouse to be involved with the partner's recovery from betrayal.

9. Advocate for new staff psychological evaluation that includes instruments that indicate personality disorders, deception, conflict management problems, marital communication problems and patterns of sexual sin.

10. Include a unit on the theology of healthy sexuality in staff orientation and/or employee handbook. Discuss frankly the probability of increased sexual temptation

due to stress, performance management, loneliness, dependence on computer technology, busyness and an increasingly sexualized cultural context. Discuss and facilitate the development of healthy relational and sexual boundaries.

11. Provide online resources on marriage, communication, conflict management, sexuality and workshops to members and leaders. Be prepared to mentor couples along the fault lines of their fractured sexuality. Encourage and enable monthly, biannual and annual single and couple time away. Include marriage and family development in annual evaluations. Include personal, couple and family development indices on annual missionary evaluation forms. Always assess marital communication and sexuality issues at debriefings.

12. Develop policies and procedures that address a full continuum of sexual behaviors. Expect deception, secrecy, resistance and trickling disclosure. Include restoration policies that address the wounded spouse, the children, team members and the church. Develop interagency collaboration for sharing policies and procedures.

13. Offer and provide as needed and requested a listening, non-judgmental presence to the offended one. Become their prayer warrior. Provide help and referrals for work around issues of emotional detachment, boundary setting, empowerment and connection with others.

14. Be careful of the tendency to label or judge the betrayed wife. Be aware of feelings and attitudes that indicate a possible misuse of

power or a denial of sexual sin. Do not compare, quantify, or minimize the woman's experience of marital sexual betrayal. Refer to another staff member or leader in cases of negative countertransference.

15. Be prepared to usher the congregation through a grief response to the betrayal by of one of their leaders or workers. Seek consultation, as needed, in the process. Facilitate transparent dialogue and the facilitated expression of anger, grief and loss within the congregation.

16. Build trust with the individual offended. Ask permission before any information is shared. Include the betrayed person and intentionally recruit female participants in all stages of discipline, care and restoration. Take into consideration as much as possible the couple's feelings about care team formation.

17. Receive anger and grief without judgment, fixing, or siding. Avoid triangulation and splitting. Allow time to pace recovery, recognizing that it may be a very long process.

18. Respect the parent's need to protect the children. Work towards transparency and full disclosure, knowing that children are often aware of painful secrets and tend to blame themselves.

19. Be a source of practical helps. Recruit members to provide meals, babysitting, grocery shopping, visiting and phone calls. Provide pastoral care. Share spiritual formation books. Provide safe housing and financial help as needed and available.

20. Invite the couple into worship without expecting any participation. Allow each of them to pace attendance and involvement. Encourage attendance at another worship community during the first months if it will help recovery.

21. Teach and preach regularly on a theology of sexuality, the effects of the fall and the process of healing. Keep up to date resources in your office and library.

22. Provide regular marriage seminars and workshops. Address openly issues of sexuality, sexual immorality in leadership and questions that emerge from a sexualized culture. Provide funding for missionary singles' and couples' retreats biannually.

23. The "failure" of the church in my research revolved around an inadequate theology of suffering, sin and evil, sexuality and healing. The church was ill-equipped to diagnose sin and to discern deception and repentance. The church was ill-prepared to structure a Spirit-led, individualized process of discipline. The shock of betrayal tested the church's ecclesiology and theology of grace, hope and restoration. The hermeneutics of headship, authority, leadership and submission may have facilitated a conscious or unconscious tendency to protect and believe the husband and to distrust and blame the wife. Churches and mission organizations lacked policies and procedures that emerged from a theology of healthy sexuality and restoration.

24. Biblical ecclesiology is replete with the "one another's" of mutual care. Matters of sexual sin are not kept in the dark, nor is the discipline process

punitive or fear-based. The church functions as a community of sinners, saved by grace, operating in gentleness and working towards restoration, unity, and healing. The church's process of discipline is modeled in the Lord's discipling of his church (Heb. 12:4-13).

Scripture and betrayal

God understands betrayal. He uses the metaphor of adultery and fornication to express His anguish and wrath over our rejection of Him in preference to small and empty idols (Jer. 2:5; Ezek. 8:12). He mourns over our hardheartedness and proclaims His enduring love in the midst of betrayal, hypocrisy, and deception (see Hos. 1:2-3a, 2:2-3, 3:1-3, 5b-8, 13-15a, 16, 19-20; Jer. 3:4-10; Ezek. 16:1-16). Our unique experience of betrayal enables us to know and understand in an intimate way God's pain as the betrayed One.

Jesus is our example in betrayal. Sexual betrayal is not the unforgiveable sin. In the New Testament, adultery was brought to a new position. Men and women were held to the same standards (Mt. 5:32; Mark 10:10-12; Luke 16:18). The very desire or willingness to commit the act was equated with adultery itself. Jesus says in Matthew 5:17-20 and 27-28: "You have heard that it was said, 'Do not commit adultery.' But I tell you that anyone who looks at a woman lustfully has already committed adultery with her in his heart." Jesus severely condemned adultery, even on the level of thought life. However, as serious as adultery was, it was not beyond forgiveness.

In John 13, we are given a model of response to betrayal. In words that echo David's heart in Psalm 55, Jesus says, "He who shares my bread has lifted up his heel against me." His betrayer was intimately acquainted with Him. Knowing who He was and where He was going, Jesus knew that His "time had come" to leave this world and go to the Father. "Having loved his own who were in the world . . . [Jesus] now showed them the full extent of his love." He washed their feet in humble service. "Now that I, your Lord and Teacher, have washed your feet, you also should wash one another's feet. I have set you an example that you should do as I have done for you" (John 13: 1-5, 14).

Jesus knew betrayal to its depths. Because of His position in the Father's love, He was able to love to the end. In 1 Peter 2:20-24, Jesus provides the model for response to the betrayal of unjust suffering, the center of healing that is based on the theology of the cross:

> For it is commendable if a man bears up under the pain of unjust suffering because he is conscious of God. But how is it to your credit if you receive a beating for doing wrong and endure it? But if you suffer for doing good and you endure it, this is commendable before God. To this you were called, because Christ suffered for you, leaving you an example, that you should follow in his steps. "He committed no sin, and no deceit was found in his mouth." When they hurled their insults at him, he did not retaliate; when he suffered, he made no threats. Instead, he entrusted himself to him who judges justly. He himself bore our sins in his body on the tree, so that we might die to sins and live by righteousness; by his wounds you have been healed.

Betrayal is especially painful when a loved one commits the giving over and delivering up. It is forged in deceit and treachery. Its consequences are feelings and experiences of unjust suffering. It is an experience known by God in the OT metaphors of broken covenant relationship, in David by the betrayal of his close companion and in Jesus by Judas' betrayal and the turning away of all his disciples. The pain of betrayal, especially the closest intimacy of marital sexual betrayal, cries out for Christ's healing.

In John 8:3-11, Jesus released the woman caught in the act of adultery from her penalty of death by stoning.

To suppose that adultery . . . stands beyond the reach of divine mercy, [or] exists as an exemption to God's provision of absolute grace, and justifies merciless judgment is to entertain rank heresy. If the gospel of grace cannot deal with adultery, it is too inept to cope with any form of immorality. If mercy is not for all sinners, persons obviously unworthy to receive mercy, it is not for any sinners. [8]

In sexual betrayal, forgiveness is one process and trust is a different process. Restoration for both the offended and the offender is needed. It is possible for the betrayed to become the betrayer[9] as they hold the other in a kind of emotional blackmail of shame. Scripture provides two clear messages about sexual immorality. It is abhorrent to God and it is forgivable. It calls forth grace and forgiveness in the context of enduring judicial, psychological and relational consequences. It breaks the most profound intimacy between man and wife that reflects the communion of the Trinity. It causes pain akin to God's pain and wrath at the faithless response of his people to his covenant of love.

Betrayal and healing

The New Testament has several different words for healing. *Iaomai* means to cure or restore--from sin, its consequences and a broken heart. The sense is of healing psychologically, of being made whole, to be free from evil. *Apokathistemi* also means to restore, to deliver from a wrong state to rightful ownership or purpose. It is a remaking to wholeness and God's created intention. This is the kind of healing that God can provide in the face of betrayal for both the betrayed and the betrayer.

God incarnate, the beloved Son, bore the full burden of deepest rejection and betrayal on the Cross. Christ entered into it with His arms wide open, entrusting Himself to God, who alone judges righteously (1 Pt. 2:23). Continual dependence on the Father enabled Him to endure the Cross. Jesus's response to deception, betrayal and unjust suffering provides a model for those wounded by sexual betrayal.

Christ's rejection and betrayal, and his acceptance and forgiveness, are a profound mystery that the betrayed and the betrayer will never be able to plumb. His model provides the guide ropes to follow on the treacherous journey of healing and restoration. He reassures that He understands and that He will never leave nor forsake (Heb. 13:5).

The forgiveness of Christ was not equated with trust, because even as Jesus forgave, knowing what was in the heart of man, He entrusted himself to no man (John 2:24-25). The betrayed are thrust into the arms of the forgiving Lord. Their heart will need to cling to Him lest they be drawn to unforgiveness and bitterness (Heb. 12:15). The betrayed easily becomes the betrayer without a reality grounding of their hopeless lostness without God's grace.

The betrayer also clings to the Lord lest they be drawn to despair or the downward spiral of habitual sin and deception. The betrayed and the betrayer sing together "Prone to wander, Lord I feel it, prone to leave the God I love." True and habitual repentance enables the full circle of betrayal's forgiveness in restoration and reconciliation.

The concept of healing in Scripture is wholistic--physical, emotional, psychological, relational and spiritual. It is God who heals. He heals thoroughly to a state of wellbeing (shalom). Jesus demonstrated this in His earthly ministry. His healing was not restricted by geographic proximity or distance, by physical contact or the lack of it, by shame and uncleanness, by social ostracism and hiddenness, or by the length and depth of the experienced disease or demonic possession. Jesus's healing was only restricted by a lack of faith. Men and women who have known sexual betrayal are called to courage to receive by faith the Lord's healing touch.

Reflection: *What has your experience with betrayal been? Have you experienced sexual betrayal? Take time to open this up before the Lord again and to ask Him for even greater healing. Have you been the betrayer through pornography or other kinds of infidelity? Take time to confess your sins before God and a trusted other that you might continue to walk in repentance and growing integrity. How can you help your staff, congregation or organization better deal with betrayal? Does your church have a restoration plan? Make one now before you need it.*

Part Five has addressed only three of the important issues facing the church which Christian leaders must address. In the urgency of changing sexual mores, the issues of singleness, sex education of our youth, and dealing with betrayal can be overlooked. Dealing with them intentionally and proactively will ensure the health of your church and future leaders.

Conclusion

"'I am the LORD, your Holy One, the Creator of Israel, your King."
Thus says the LORD, who makes a way through the sea and a path
through the mighty waters…. "Do not call to mind the former
things, or ponder things of the past. Behold, I will do something
new, now it will spring forth; will you not be aware of it? I will even
make a roadway in the wilderness, rivers in the desert.'"
(Is. 43:15-19)

Almost every day I hear stories about sexual problems among
Christian leaders. Just this week, two pastors' wives wrote me
about their concerns. This volume cannot contain all the needs
and all the ways that we are wounded, nor all of our ignorance
and the ways that we wound. But I pray that it is a start. I hope
that it has given you some language to understand yourself, your
loved ones and your congregation or organization. I hope that you
are enabled to start talking more openly about sexuality. Sex is
God's divine plan.

I want to close our discussion with some implications for your
church or organization.

First, we need to work towards a cohesive biblical theology of
sexuality. We need to search the Scriptures and interact with
existing theologies. We need to listen to and talk with each other.
How can we welcome those with beliefs different than our own?
How can we welcome and accept and still hold true to Scripture?
How can we hold true to Scripture and yet still offer love and
acceptance? It seems to me that it all comes down to this question
and we tend to err on one side or the other. Either we hold to our
biblical understandings of Scripture and reject the different (i.e.
the LGBTQ+ community), or we accept and welcome and diminish
the centrality of Scripture. I have not met those who do this walk

well and follow a solid Jesus middle way of grace and truth. We need to be teachable. We need to repent of abandoning truth for fear of appearing unloving or intolerant. We need to repent of our critical, judgmental spirits as we have excluded those different from us.

Second, we must not let confusion about what is right, accusations of intolerance or fears about God's reputation silence us and keep us from teaching and preaching and writing on sexuality. Our children are being faced with beliefs and choices that we want to protect them from but cannot. God has called us to such a time as this. Our children, youth and young adults need support and help in their decision-making and life choices. Our singles need affirmation and community. Our marriages need strengthening. Our LGBTQ+ individuals need respect and belonging.

I remember a meeting with David Augsburger, author of more than twenty books on pastoral counseling.[1] He spoke with us about his area's clergy group. They had made a commitment to mention the issue of sexual abuse from the pulpit at least once annually. These pastors were amazed by the extraordinary response from their congregations. So many individuals were eager to talk about areas of their lives that had been cloaked in shame! Too often we leaders are silent when our culture and media and peers are quite loud with alternative ways of educating.

The Bible is full of instruction and examples about sexuality. Let's make sure that it is a regular topic of discussion and that we have curricula in our seminaries and mission training schools. We need developed sex education programs for children, youth, young adults, marrieds and singles, male and female, seniors, etc., so that the world is not the main source of (mis)information. Let's make sure to share the materials that we develop through online communities and publication. Our libraries should have available resources in all the pertinent areas. Let's use stories of people who have found hope and healing in their sexual journey to encourage those who walk a difficult path.

Third, we must develop policies and procedures in our organizations that reflect grace and truth. Sexual sin is one area that must be addressed, but clearly not the only one. Does our organization have electronic device filtering? Who gets the results and how are they handled? How are emotional attachments addressed? Who evaluates our lifestyle behavior? Is there a written restoration plan in place that addresses the needs of the whole family as well as the church and organization? Who is willing to serve on restoration teams of care? Do we have child protection and sexual harassment policies in place? Do we have a sexuality position paper that is readily available for those who have questions about sexual issues?

Fourth, we need to teach, lead and model a balanced life that celebrates our gendered creation in the image of God. Dr. Gloria Halverson notes that we must start somewhere. For her, it would be addressing the many that have been marginalized and wounded by Christian judgmentalism. For others, it will be to start with a theology of sexuality. We will make mistakes along the way, but God will instruct and guide, forgive and heal.

As we address the unique challenges of Christian leadership in a God-honoring way, our communities will be watching and learning. Let's commit to restoring the ancient paths with spiritual disciplines that helped keep the foundations strong: silence and solitude, fasting, tithes and offerings, prayer, honoring the Sabbath, etc.

Finally, despite all the burdens around sexuality in the intersection of faith and culture, can we agree to celebrate that this is God's very good idea and that He will help us to navigate it? Together, let's trust our incarnate, embodied Lord to lead us in paths of truth and righteousness for His name's sake.

We will be sought by believers and unbelievers alike to help navigate the very confusing landscape of sexuality in our world today. We will hear stories of terrible pain. We will work with predators and victims, with the betrayed and with some who have become betrayers. If we have not addressed our own sexual history and worked to become educated and surrendered in our own sanctification process, we may become another painful stop in someone's life. We need to be prepared, equipped and enabled. The areas of question and need grow daily, but the most common ones are addressed briefly in the Appendix.

I'm on the journey with you to glory, being restored to my creation intent in all the mystery and wonder of what that means. To God be the glory. May we be known in this confusing time as repairers of the breach, discovering God's paths together.

And your ancient ruins shall be rebuilt; you shall raise up the foundations of many generations; you shall be called the repairer of the breach, the restorer of streets to dwell in. (Is. 58:12)

.

Appendix

Some areas that are necessary for self- and other education are included below. You can add your own research to these listed and include additional issues that your church or organization is facing. Many in the Christian LGBTQ+ communities complain that we are not addressing weighty areas of sin in our congregations. Clearly, we may floodlight issues around same-sex marriage or gender transitioning, but the prominent sexuality issues in the church today that must be addressed are premarital and extramarital sex and pornography use.

- Masturbation

Masturbation is not mentioned in Scripture. Onan's practice of withdrawal to avoid inseminating his wife, received by Levirate marriage, has been used inaccurately to describe God's displeasure at masturbation (Gen. 38:9-10). In order to evaluate behaviors and practices that are not specifically identified in Scripture, it is helpful to consider biblical principles. As those set free in Christ, all things are lawful, but not all things edify. We are provided questions to ask of any behavior (1 Cor. 6:12, 9:27, 10:13, 10:23-33):

- Does it somehow disqualify me from ministry?
- Does it tempt me into other sins?
- Is it beneficial, constructive and edifying for me and others?
- Do I feel guilty about it?
- Does it master me?
- Does it glorify God?

Masturbation is frequently encouraged in couples' sex therapy to enable individuals to learn what is pleasurable so as to teach their spouse and enhance sexual intimacy. Usually, however, masturbation is a solitary practice for solitary release of sexual tension. Pitfalls include it becoming habit, it being used to avoid marital intimacy, it being a medicator to avoid dealing with feelings and coupling it with nonmarital fantasy or pornography. It promotes self-pleasuring rather than sexual pleasure as a gift to be enjoyed with the God-given other.

Masturbation has the potential of narrowing the marital experience and draining energy and focus from the marriage bed. So, get educated, review your own history and experience and determine before the Lord what is right and good in your situation. Talk and pray about it with your spouse or support network. If it has become an addictive habit or intrusive in your marriage, it might signal areas of stress, anxiety or loneliness that need to be addressed. Masturbation is often shrouded in shame in the church. We as leaders need to talk about it.

- Pornography

Pornography is a prevalent and disturbing problem in Christian leaders. I have heard all sorts of rationalizations about it that come from a kind of entitled, narcissistic base. "I need it. S/he doesn't meet my needs. S/he's too tired. I am more sexual and have greater needs. I deserve it. S/he doesn't turn me on." Harry Schaumburg (1992) describes pornography as "false intimacy." William Struthers (2010) notes that it derails God's creation of us as "wired for intimacy." Christian leaders need to be ruthlessly honest in this domain and expect the same of others through authentic accountability and strong electronic filtering systems.[1] Pornography is highly addictive.

My friend worked for years in missionary member care and learned to change the application interview question from "Have you viewed pornography in the past year?" to "When you have seen pornography, how have you handled it?" It is important to note that young women are the fastest growing population of pornography users and that the average age of a child's first exposure is eleven.[2] Our education needs to start with grade school children and extend to men and women.[3]

- Premarital sex

Premarital sex is expected and assumed in our context today and this has become the norm in the church.[4] Approximately 80% of young evangelicals have engaged in premarital sex and 1/3 of their pregnancies have ended in abortion.[5] Our "True Love Waits," "Just Say No," and abstinence-only campaigns are not working.[6] Interestingly, many, despite their behavior, still believe that premarital sex is wrong, and this causes guilt from incongruence in values and behavior.

We need to carefully evaluate Scripture and teach a healthy theology of sexuality to our youth. Rev. Nigel Genders, Chief Education Officer of the Church of England, notes that in Church of England schools, relationship and sex education "will be rooted in the teachings of the Church, including the importance of trust, loyalty, fidelity and the Christian understanding of marriage as the context for sexual relationships, as well as the understanding of abstinence and celibacy as positive life choices."[7] My husband and many of his clergy colleagues have adopted a practice requesting engaged couples to agree to a period of abstinence before marriage in order to honor and enable vows of chastity.

- Extramarital sex and divorce

In the face of dismal statistics, David French writes of the importance of "marriage restoration" in the Church.[8] 22% of married men and 14% of married women have committed adultery during their marriage.[9] Nominal conservative Protestants have a high rate of divorce, but active conservative Protestants have a 36% less likely chance of divorce, contrary to current popular belief.[10] Extramarital sex is a frequent cause of divorce. Recovery is possible but requires hard work and good help.[11]

- Abortion

Abortion cannot be undone. Many struggle with secret guilt over abortion. It is morally confusing that our culture allows and affirms abortion as our right. The good news is that abortion rates are decreasing. The bad news is that many in your church or organization will have had, enabled or forced an abortion.[12] We can take advantage of Sanctity of Human Life Sunday (SOHLS), held annually every January, to offer prayer and counseling for those who are post-abortive.[13] We can provide resources and referrals for those who request them and encourage our churches and organizations in foster care, adoption care and single parent support.[14] We can minister forgiveness for our involvement and passivity around this issue of justice.

- Same-sex desire

The rates of same sex attraction, orientation and identification are increasing.[15] According to the Kinsey Institute, about 3.5% of adults identify as gay, lesbian or bisexual and 0.3% as transgender.[16] Approximately 8.2% of adult Americans have engaged in same-sex behavior and 11% experience some level of same-sex attraction (SSA). These are helpful statistics because it means that more than 1 out of 10 people in your church or organization experiences SSA. Maybe that is you and you have felt ashamed and alone. This is an area of heightened discussion in our communities and can be very disturbing and isolating for the individual Christian feeling it.[17] Our churches and organizations need to provide good sex education for children, youth and adults to enable them to evaluate cultural messages and environmental pressures from school and media and to learn how to understand their own feelings and God's love for them.

- Gender confusion and dysphoria

Approximately 0.3% of American adults are identified as transgender, which can have a great variety of expression.

Dysphoria is the term for significant unhappiness around gender.[18] It is a clinical term that means more than just confusion. Of the children that experience gender dysphoria, 12-27% will continue into adulthood as transgender.[19] Most will grow into a degree of acceptance and satisfaction with their birth gender despite earlier confusion and unhappiness. Although this may be a small percentage of your congregation, their needs will be significant.

It seems to me that our historical stereotyping of gender and gender roles has obscured the rich and wide freedom and beauty of God's creation intent for each of us. The world sees us as inexcusably intolerant in our desire for people to live out their natal gender. We must be able to teach, explain, respect and give dignity to people all along the path of dealing with their gender feelings.[20] We have a lot more work to do to determine what it means to be created male and female.

- Sexual abuse

Sexual abuse is far more common than we realize. One in three women and one in six men have experienced some sort of sexual violence in their lifetime, with one in 5 women and one in 76 men reporting having been raped.[21] Our churches and Christian organizations need to be safe for children, men and women. We need to develop policies for protection of youth and background checks of childcare providers and teachers. We need policies about sexual harassment and how to integrate in the congregation felons with a history of sexual abuse or predation. Help and templates for policy development can be found online.

- Sex trafficking

Sex trafficking represents about 80% of the picture of modern global slavery. The average age of entry into the US sex trade is 12-14 years-old, many of whom are girls who were runaways with a history of sexual abuse.[22] Dr. Gloria Halverson, expert in sex trafficking and current president of Christian Medical and Dental

Association, notes that all of our youth are at risk; sex trafficking is "equal opportunity."[23]

Endnotes

Introduction

[1] All names and identifying information have been changed to protect confidentiality.

[2] Please see the resource list at the end of this book.

[3] To better understand deconstruction as it applies to the church and faith, see K. Giles, "The six pillars of religious deconstruction," *Patheos* (2019), https://www.patheos.com/blogs/keithgiles/2019/08/the-6-pillars-of-religious-deconstruction/

Chapter 4

[1] See http://www.soulshepherding.org/2009/11/pastors-under-stress/ for more information and resources on ministry stress. In 2009, CNN Money noted that 71% of ministers noted that their jobs were highly stressful. They are included in this article's list of highly stressed and not well-paid workers. http://money.cnn.com/galleries/2009/pf/0910/gallery.stressful_jobs/10.html Missionary stress is a well-known phenomenon and is a frequent topic addressed at Mental Health and Missions conferences https://www.mti.org/conferences/mental-health-and-missions/. For a summary on missionary stress, see http://www.missionarycare.com/stewardship-stress.html

[2] All the Townsend and Cloud Boundary books are helpful in this area, e.g. *Boundaries, Boundaries in marriage, Boundaries with kids, Boundaries in dating*. Also see C. R. Benyei, *When a congregation is betrayed: Responding to clergy misconduct* (Rowman & Littlefield Publishers, 2005).

[3] I remember a student telling me with pride how he took his wife on all of his pastoral visits to the suffering and grieving. I wondered if his wife minded serving as his chastity belt. Ruthless self-awareness is crucial to develop your unique safeguards.

[4] E. Stetzer, "Accountability Questions," *Christianity Today* (2008). http://www.christianitytoday.com/edstetzer/2008/may/accountability-questions.html

[5] Between 57 and 64% of male pastors struggle with pornography. https://www.christiantoday.com/article/57-percent-of-pastors-and-64-of-youth-pastors-in-u-s-struggle-with-porn-addiction-survey-shows/78178.htm. In contrast, about 13% of Christian women struggle with pornography, but individual therapists give a higher percentage. https://www.cru.org/us/en/train-and-grow/life-and-relationships/are-

we-failing-christian-women-in-the-battle-against-porn.html. These percentages are likely underestimated.

Chapter 5

[1] This is part of the reason that Just Between Us, a resource for ministry women, was developed https://justbetweenus.org/. Ron and Bonnie Koteskey have a wonderful online resource for missionaries, http://www.missionarycare.com/.

[2] Ravi Zacharias calls this a "minefield of sensitivities" in his YouTube talk, (2019), https://www.youtube.com/watch?list=RD92I9EBYLseQ&v=92I9EBYLseQ

[3] See https://www.aacc.net/, https://www.christiancounselordirectory.com/ and https://www.restoredhopenetwork.org/

Chapter 6

[1] Situation ethics is "the position that moral decision making is contextual or dependent on a set of circumstances. Situation ethics holds that moral judgments must be made within the context of the entirety of a situation and that all normative features of a situation must be viewed as a whole. The guiding framework for moral decision making is stated variously as that of acting in the most loving way, to maximize harmony and reduce discord, or to enrich human existence" https://www.britannica.com/topic/situation-ethics. See J. F. Fletcher, *Situation ethics: The new morality* (Westminster John Knox Press, 1966).

[2] See T. S Sellers, *Sex, God & the conservative Church: Erasing shame from sexual intimacy* (Routledge, 2017).

[3] Body dysmorphic disorder is a psychiatric diagnosis of preoccupation and unhappiness with the body or body parts. Gender dysphoria, also a psychiatric disorder, is a profound unhappiness with birth gender.

[4] Living Waters is an international program of healing sexual and relational brokenness. Groups are held within and under the direction of the local church. The ministry focuses on listening healing prayer and is facilitated by trained lay leaders. For more information, see https://desertstream.org/living-waters/.

Chapter 7

[1] Sellers writes of her work with Christians in therapy, "Much of ... sexual suffering was generally rooted in either of two primary venues.... One was a culture of silence or of punishment around forms of sexual curiosity, and the other was a social culture that defined sex and the body as objects for pleasure without any consideration for relationship and mutual care.... Both men and women expressed feeling ashamed of

their sexual desires or experiences. They told long histories of seeing sexual desire as something wrong, impure, or problematic, about them. Women described a sense of disdain for their bodies—how they looked, how they felt, their desire or lack of it. Men spoke about feeling entitled to sex and then disappointment in their sexual relationships, or a sense of confusion and naivete around what to expect from their partner, or even around rudimentary skills like how to love, how to touch, or what was needed to bring their partner pleasure. In nearly all cases, there was an obvious lack of grounding in any form of sex education—positive or spiritually rooted...." (Sellers, 4).

[2] Living Waters program addresses the effects of misogyny and misandry in detail. See A. Comiskey, *Restoring relational integrity through the broken body of Christ* (2013). Available through Desert Streams Living Waters.

Chapter 8

[1] S. Wunderink, "Reading the world" (2007), http://www.christianitytoday.com/ct/2007/octoberweb-only/142-22.0.html?start=1.

[2] E. Goodman, "Cultural exegesis" (2010), http://missionsmisunderstood.com/2010/03/09/cultural-exegesis/

[3] Many of us will not be able to engage as rapidly and deeply as is urgently needed. I have provided a resource list at the end of this book to help you educate yourself. I recommend reading the cultural and theological selections first.

[4] Perhaps the well-known hymn by Charlotte Elliot (1935) expresses it best, "Just as I am," sung at the end of Billy Graham Crusades to welcome any all that need Jesus to come:

Just as I am -- without one plea/ But that Thy blood was shed for me,/ And that Thou bidst me come to Thee,/ O Lamb of God, I come!

Just as I am and waiting not/ To rid my soul of one dark blot,/ To Thee, whose blood can cleanse each spot,/ O Lamb of God, I come!

Just as I am though toss'd about/ With many a conflict, many a doubt,/ Fightings and fears within, without,/ O Lamb of God, I come!

Just as I am poor, wretched, blind;/ Sight, riches, healing of the mind,/ Yea, all I need, in Thee to find,/ O Lamb of God, I come!

Just as I am Thou wilt receive,/ Wilt welcome, pardon, cleanse, relieve;/ Because Thy promise I believe, O Lamb of God, I come!

Just as I am Thy love unknown/ Has broken every barrier down;/ Now to be Thine, yea, Thine alone,
O Lamb of God, I come!

Just as I am of that free love/ The breadth, length, depth, and height to prove,/ Here for a season, then above,/ O Lamb of God, I come! https://en.wikipedia.org/wiki/Just_As_I_Am_(hymn)

[5] "The Lord was standing beside a wall built with a plumb line, with a plumb line in his hand. And the LORD said to me, 'Amos, what do you see?' And I said, 'A plumb line.' Then the Lord said, 'Behold, I am setting a plumb line in the midst of my people Israel: I will never again pass by them; the high places of Isaac shall be made desolate, and the sanctuaries of Israel shall be laid waste, and I will rise against the house of Jeroboam with the sword'" (Amos 7:8-9).

Chapter 9

[1] Mel Lawrenz understands this as a crucial need of our times, *A time for dignity: Crisis and gospel today* (WordWay, 2015).

[2] See A. Bloom's classic book, *The closing of the American mind. How higher education has failed democracy and impoverished the souls of today's students* (Simon and Schuster,2012) and O. Guinness, *Renaissance: The power of the gospel however dark the times* (IVP, 2014).

[3] These two books by Yarhouse are important reading to understand our culture: *Understanding gender dysphoria: Navigating transgender issues in a changing culture* (IVP, 2015), and M.A. Yarhouse & E.S.N. Tan, *Sexuality and sex therapy: A comprehensive Christian appraisal* (IVP, 2014).

[4] For a full exposition of the integrity lens, see R. A. J. Gagnon, *The Bible and homosexual practice: Texts and hermeneutics* (Abingdon Press, 2002).

[5] See C. Plantinga, Jr., *Not the way it's supposed to be: A breviary of sin* (Eerdmans, 1996).

[6] M. A. Yarhouse. 2015. https://www.christianitytoday.com/ct/2015/july-august/understanding-transgender-gender-dysphoria.html.

[7] Ibid. See also work by Justin Lee to better understand the diversity lens, *Torn: Rescuing the Gospel from the Gay vs. Christian debate* (Jericho Books, 2013).

[8] Ravi Zacharias suggests that we add a fourth lens, "transversity," the transcendent truth of what is ultimate applied to what is transient. (2019), https://www.youtube.com/watch?list=RD92I9EBYLseQ&v=92I9EBYLseQ

Chapter 10

[1] See C. H. J. Wright, *The mission of God: Unlocking the Bible's grand narrative* (IVP, 2006).

[2] Personal correspondence, 11/20/17.

[3] H. Whelchel, "The four-chapter Gospel: The grand metanarrative told by the Bible" (The Institute for Faith, Work & Economics, 2012), https://tifwe.org/the-four-chapter-gospel-the-grand-metanarrative-told-by-the-bible/

[4] I am deeply indebted to Eastbrook Church and Senior Pastor Matt Erickson and Pastors Jim Caler and Ruth Carver. We prayed, worked, edited and considered difficult questions together. This biblical theology of sexuality of Part Four is drawn from our initial position paper. It is used with permission.

Chapter 11

[1] Though rare, intersex and genetic disorders of sexual development do exist and may require additional consideration and prayerful guidance.

[2] For a detailed journey through Scripture on homosexuality, explaining different interpretations and historical evidence, see Preston Sprinkle, *People to be loved: Why homosexuality is not just an issue* (Zondervan, 2015).

Chapter 13

[1] See Ronald Rolheiser, *The holy longing: The search for a Christian spirituality* (Crown Publishing Group, 2014).

[2] M. J. Dawn, *Sexual character* (Wm. B. Eerdmans, 1993).

Chapter 15

[1] This course was taught with Dr. Daniel Green through the Wisconsin Center for Christian Study and Trinity Evangelical Divinity School at Elmbrook Church in 2015. Thanks to Dr. Douglas Rosenau who also informed this assessment tool.

Chapter 16

[1] You may be confused by the multitude of help available. Psychiatrists are MDs (medical doctors) that are able to evaluate, diagnose and treat. Psychologists have PhDs or PsyDs and are involved in research, evaluation, diagnosis and treatment. Then there are mastered level providers and this is a good place to start—MSW, MSN, MA. There are addiction specialists, LPCs (licensed professional counselors) and lay counselors. Don't be afraid to ask questions and to explore options to find the best fit for you and your situation. There are Christian support groups like Celebrate Recovery or Living Waters. There are confidential 12-step groups like Sex Anonymous (SA) or Sex-Anon for spouses and many other options of help. There is also the possibility of online individual or group counseling in your area of need. This is particularly helpful for those living overseas.

² See *The healing path: How the hurts in your past can lead you to a more abundant life* (WaterBrook, 2000) and *Healing the wounded heart: The heartache of sexual abuse and the hope of transformation* (BakerBooks, 2016). Other resources are noted on Allendar's website, https://theallendercenter.org

³ https://www.focusonthefamily.com/search-results#q=sexual%20abuse%20recovery&t=FocusOnTheFamilyOnly&sort=relevancy

⁴ Compassion fatigue is secondary traumatization that caregivers and first responders may experience as they hear stories of trauma repeatedly. In sexual abuse recovery, an individual may need to talk and share over time their own story until they "get it right." Friends and family may not be able to continue listening over the long haul.

⁵"All other sins a person commits are outside the body, but whoever sins sexually, sins against their own body" (1 Cor. 6:15). I believe that this is part of the mystery of our sexuality and the core of our identity. This doesn't negate the charge against us that, even as the Lord says in Mt. 23:23, we may have ignored the weightier matters in our quick judgment of sexual sin, "Woe to you, scribes and Pharisees, hypocrites! For you tithe mint and dill and cumin, and have neglected the weightier matters of the law: justice and mercy and faithfulness. These you ought to have done, without neglecting the others."

⁶For marriage and the Trinity, see https://www.reviveourhearts.com/radio/revive-our-hearts/marriage-and-the-trinity/, for Christ and the Church, Gal. 2:24 and 28, https://www.desiringgod.org/articles/a-metaphor-of-christ-and-the-church, and for community and intimacy https://kineticmin.wordpress.com/2014/10/04/marriage-a-reflection-of-the-trinity/.

⁷ God giving us over as a consequence of our sin is an important aspect of His judgment and certainly a factor in besetting sins and addictions.

⁸ Ps. 115:4-8, Ps. 135:15-18; Rom. 1:18-27. See G. K. Beale, *We become what we worship: A biblical theology of idolatry* (IVP, 2008).

⁹ See P. D. Jamieson, *The face of forgiveness: A pastoral theology of shame and redemption* (IVP, 2016).

¹⁰ See L. Payne, *Restoring the Christian soul: Overcoming barriers to completion in Christ through healing prayer* (Baker Books, 1996).

[11] Meditate on and memorize Ps. 139 to internalize the truth that God knows you completely and that nothing is too dark for Him.

Chapter 17

[1] A. A. Calhoun, in her *Spiritual disciplines handbook: Practices that transform us* (IVP, 2015) pairs spiritual disciplines with spiritual needs.

Chapter 19

[1] B. DePaolo. "What has changed for single Americans in the past decade?" (2016), https://www.washingtonpost.com/news/soloish/wp/2016/09/20/what-has-changed-for-single-americans-in-the-past-decade/

[2] https://www.statista.com/topics/999/singles/, June 2018.

[3] Ibid.

[4] Further trends are noted: "As the nation's household and family structure continues to change and median age at first marriage rises, the proportion of young adults who are married has decreased. In 2018, 29 percent of young adults ages 18 to 34 were married, a decrease of 30 percentage points when compared to 59 percent of young adults being married in 1978. Along with changes in the age of first marriage and marriage rates, there have been changes in the number of young adults living with an unmarried partner. In 2018, 15 percent of young adults ages 25 to 34 lived with an unmarried partner, up from 12 percent in 2008. Among those ages 18 to 24, cohabitation is now more prevalent than living with a spouse; 9 percent of these young adults lived with an unmarried partner, compared to 7 percent who lived with a spouse in 2018." https://www.census.gov/newsroom/press-releases/2018/families.html

[5] F. Friday. https://observer.com/2018/01/more-americans-are-single-than-ever-before-and-theyre-healthier-too/

[6] Interview with Nic Fridenmaker, Director of High School Ministry at Eastbrook Church, Milwaukee, WI on 1/16/2020.

[7] As quoted in H. Wraight, *Single: The Jesus Model* (Wheaton: Crossway, 1987).

[8] Liz Carver enlarges the NT new understanding of family:

> But in the New Testament, family takes on a deeper theological meaning. Time and again the point is made that while we are all born into physical families at birth, when we surrender our lives to Christ, we are adopted into a new spiritual family (Romans 8:15). Jesus demonstrates this when he calls his spiritual family his "mother and brothers," even when his actual blood relatives are waiting outside (Matthew 12:46-50). The Gospel of John

reinforces the prioritization of spiritual children over natural-born children (John 1:12-13). The Apostle Paul writes of identity in Galatians, calling all who put their faith in Christ "children" of God, setting aside identity markers such as Jew/Gentile, slave/free, male/female for the sake of unity in Christ through faith (Galatians 3:27-28). Finally, in the book of Revelation, John describes a heavenly vision of people from "every nation, tribe, people, and language" worshipping together, unified in their vocational call to worship the same God (Revelation 7:9-10). Taken from L. Carver, "Calling the Church to return to a theology of singleness," (Unpublished manuscript submitted to Fuller Theological Seminary, 2017). Used with permission of the author.

[9] Erica Breitbarth, message notes, used by permission.

[10] Carver.

[11] See Doug Rosenau's *Soul Virgin* for answers to these specific questions.

[12] Carver.

[13] Ibid.

[14] Carver concludes,

> A theology of singleness rejects the pervasive idolatry of marriage, happiness, and fitting in and instead calls individuals to find their belonging and value in who God says they are. Individuals with a theology of singleness are marked by their wholehearted devotion to God (1 Corinthians 7), an identity found solely in God (Colossians 3:3), and their commitment to love and serve the diverse family of God (Revelation 7). Individuals with a theology of singleness have an integrated view of sexuality, a high view of celibacy and a realistic view of both marriage and marital sexuality. They rightly value solitude, vulnerability, and self-trust as the keys to self-acceptance, and their self-acceptance fuels the flow of love from God through themselves, out to the community. Finally, individuals with a theology of singleness do the hard work of properly ordering their desires in a way that prioritizes God over personal pleasure, which requires that they walk through the world in a posture of humility.

Chapter 20

[1] The International Center for Transgender Care notes a dramatic rise in gender dysphoria in children. "This change is likely due to an increase in awareness of the condition, as well as an increase in family and societal

support for gender nonconforming children, rather than an increase in the condition itself." https://thetranscenter.com/holistic-therapy/gender-dysphoria-in-children/ There has also been an increase in reporting same sex attraction in younger people. See https://www.livescience.com/53288-younger-people-report-same-sex-attractions.html.

[2] K. D. Whitehead, (1996), "Sex education: The Vatican's guidelines." https://www.catholiceducation.org/en/marriage-and-family/sexuality/sex-education-the-vatican-s-guidelines.html

[3] Ibid.

[4] https://mps.milwaukee.k12.wi.us/MPS-English/CAO/Documents/Health-Education/MPSHGD1stgradecurriculum2014-15.pdf

[5] https://mps.milwaukee.k12.wi.us/MPS-English/CAO/Documents/Health-Education/MPSHGD4thgradecurriculum2014-15.pdf

[6] https://mps.milwaukee.k12.wi.us/MPS-English/CAO/Documents/Health-Education/MPSHGD7thGradecurriculum2014-2015.pdf

[7] https://www.catholiceducation.org/en/marriage-and-family/sexuality/sex-education-the-vatican-s-guidelines.html.

[8] Ibid.

[9] Laure Herlinger is Pastoral Senior Director of Next Gen Ministry at Eastbrook Church, Milwaukee, WI. Eastbrook is a diverse urban church of about 1100 members and 1600 weekly attendance. Next Gen covers infancy through high school age children. Interview 1/16/2020.

[10] Interview with Leslie Osborne, 1/16/2020, former pastor of Children and Family Ministry at Eastbrook Church, Milwaukee Wisconsin.

[11] Interview with Janis Ryder, 1/16/2020, Elmbrook Church Lake Country, Delafield, WI, a suburb of Milwaukee. Ryder was also children's pastor of Mamlaka Church in Nairobi, Kenya for many years.

[12] N. Fridenmaker interview, 1/16/2020.

[13] See B. Butler and J. and C. Evert, You. Life, love, and the theology of the body (Ascension Press, 2016). For teens. Leaders Guide, Student Guide, Parent Guide and 5-dvd set are available.

[14] Katie (2014) writes that

> Abstinence is an aspect of pre-marital chastity but isn't the endgame. Chastity runs much deeper by giving us a deep reverence and respect for both our eternal souls and the heart

of God. Loving someone never means sinning with them. Whether you are single, married or ordained you too are called to honor God through your body. https://chastity.com/2014/05/chastity-before-marriage-fosters-chastity-in-marriage/

[15]C. Cole, (2015), https://www.thegospelcoalition.org/article/rethinking-sex-ed-in-the-church/

[16] Ibid.

Chapter 21

[1] L. Sinclair, *Shattered dreams and shattered vows: The lived experience of healing marital sexual betrayal in North American Missionary Women*, (A dissertation submitted to Columbia Seminary & School of Missions, Columbia, SC, 2010).

[2] Today we can add a fourth "A" because many young people are exposed to pornography by Accident.

[3] Most of the women in my research described difficulty in trusting male church leaders after their husband's betrayal. This would be an important dynamic to explore in pastoral counseling.

[4] True repentance is a gift of God (2 Tim. 2:25). It includes godly sorrow for the sin (2 Cor 7:10) and a turning to Him with fruits of repentance (Mt. 3:8).

[5] This may be counterintuitive. It is very helpful for those who have experienced betrayal to realize that their recovery may take longer than they expected, and longer than their mate's.

[6] It is not unusual for betrayed partners to monitor communications, phones, credit cards, gas mileage, use of time, etc. in order to know if their spouse is "cheating."

[7] There is no bonding relationship with pornography, but rather a multitude of fantasy images against which there is no competition.

[8] C. W. Gaddy, *Adultery & grace: The ultimate scandal*. (Grand Rapids, MI: William B. Eerdmans Publishing Company, 1996) p. 8.

[9] Dan Allender and Tremper Longman provide a wonderful explanation of the betrayed becoming the betrayer in *Bold Love* (NavPress, 2014).

Conclusion

[1] See https://www.amazon.com/s?k=david+augsburger&ref=nb_sb_noss.

Appendix

[1] Covenant Eyes has individual and organizational filtering programs with educational assistance. See https://www.covenanteyes.com/resources-for-pastors/. There are many other filter options available but I find their

built-in accountability system and educational support very helpful. Remember to make this a part of your employee interviews, including females. Children's exposure will be ever younger.

[2] https://www.challies.com/articles/10-ugly-and-updated-numbers-about-pornography-use/

[3] My husband's dissertation research was on helping North American missionary men remain sexually pure. He described the "way forward" as six paving stones: 1. Perseverance, 2. Connection and community, 3. Accountability with others, 4. Self-awareness, understanding and examination, 5. Exercise, sleep, Sabbath rest and nutrition, and 6. Spiritual disciplines. P. L. Sinclair, *Factors influencing North American missionary men to remain sexually pure* (Dissertation submitted to Columbia Biblical Seminary and School of Missions, Columbia, SC, 2008).

[4] The increased rates of divorce that are linked to premarital sex need to be part of our premarital teaching.

[5] https://www.huffpost.com/entry/evangelicals-sex-frank-talk_n_1443062, https://www.webmd.com/sex-relationships/news/20061220/premarital-sex-the-norm-in-america

[6] Lawrence B. Finer, *Trends in premarital sex in the United States* (2007), https://www.ncbi.nlm.nih.gov/pmc/articles/PMC1802108/ notes that premarital sex is "normative" behavior and has been for the past 50 years. "These findings argue for education and interventions that provide young people with the skills and information they need to protect themselves from unintended pregnancy and sexually transmitted diseases once they become sexually active."

[7] As reported by Eleanor Busby in *The Independent* (3/12/18), "Pupils should be taught in school that abstinence and celibacy are 'positive life choices', says Church of England."

[8] https://www.nationalreview.com/corner/evangelicals-collapsing-sexual-mores-david-french/

[9] http://www.divorcestatistics.info/latest-infidelity-statistics-of-usa.html

[10] https://www.christianitytoday.com/edstetzer/2014/february/marriage-divorce-and-body-of-christ-what-do-stats-say-and-c.html See also S. Feldhahn, *The surprising secrets of highly happy marriages: The little things that make a big difference* (Multnomah, 2013).

[11] Kathy Schoenborn LPC teaches the marriage statistics that 15% of couples never should have married due to abuse, etc. 15% have found their soulmate and 70% are on a continuum of working at their marriage.

[12] In 2014, approximately 19% of all US pregnancies ended in abortion. In the 70s, the rate was as high as 1/3 to 1/4 of all pregnancies. https://abort73.com

[13] Resources can be found at https://lifechoices.org/sanctity-of-human-life-sunday/

[14] See https://ramahinternational.org/ and L. Cochrane, *Forgiven and set free: A post-abortion Bible study for women* (Baker Books, 2015). Cochrane and Kathy Jones also have written a book for men, *Healing a father's heart: a post-abortion study for men.*

[15] https://www.cdc.gov/nchs/data/nhsr/nhsr036.pdf

[16] https://kinseyinstitute.org/research/faq.php

[17] See books by Mark Yarhouse in Resource List to increase education and understanding.

[18] The Christian Medical and Dental Association has excellent position papers on areas of sexual concern including homosexuality, transgender, reproductive technology, etc. https://cmda.org/position-statements/

[19] https://kinseyinstitute.org/research/faq.php. See Mark Yarhouse on gender dysphoria for clarification of definitions around gender confusion and dysphoria and transgender attractions.

[20] During the 20-week Living Waters program, we address gender stereotypes and the goodness of our God-given gender. In small group one evening, the women wrote words that had been spoken over them: incapable, worthless, a whore just like your mother, too needy, made to meet man's needs, controlling, manipulative, angry, too emotional, too intense, too fat, too ugly, too stupid, too complicated, too much, arm candy, demanding, you should have been a boy. The men's small group did the same: invisible, too small, too weak, too passive, you don't have what it takes, you'll never be good enough, you aren't enough, you're so pretty you should be a girl, your eyelashes are so long that you're a pretty girl, you're not intelligent like your wife.

[21] https://www.nsvrc.org/node/4737

[22] https://www.dosomething.org/us/facts/11-facts-about-human-trafficking. There are several organizations that your community can join to support the battle against trafficking. See https://faastinternational.org/about-us/our-mission.

[23] Personal conversation, 6/9/19.

Resource List

Culture

Collins, N. 2017. *All but invisible: Exploring identity questions at the intersection of faith, gender and sexuality.* Zondervan.

Hirsch, D. 2015. *Redeeming sex: Naked conversations about sexuality and spirituality.* IVP.

Hollinger, D. P. 2009. *The Meaning of sex: Christian ethics and the moral life.* Grand Rapids, MI: Baker Academic.

Paris, J. W. 2011. *The end of sexual identity: Why sex is too important to define who we are.* Downers Grove, IL: InterVarsity Press.

Pearcey, N. R. 2018. *Love thy body: Answering hard questions about life and sexuality.* Grand Rapids, MI: BakerBooks.

_____. 2008. *Total truth: Liberating Christianity from its cultural captivity.* Wheaton, IL: Crossway.

Shalit, W. 2007. *Girls gone mild: Young women reclaim self-respect and find it's not bad to be good.* New York: Random House.

Smith, W. J. 2016. *The Culture of Death: The Age of Do No Harm Medicine.* Encounter Books.

Walls, J. L., Neill, J. and D. Baggett, eds. 2018. *Venus and Virtue: Celebrating Sex and Seeking Sanctification.* Eugene, OR: Cascade Books.

Theology

Ash, C. 2005. *Marriage in the Service of God*. Vancouver, BC: Regent College Publishing.

Butterfield, R. C. 2015. *Openness Unhindered: Further Thoughts of an Unlikely Convert on Sexual Identity and Union with Christ*. Pittsburgh: Crown & Covenant.

Danylak, B. 2007. *A Biblical Theology of Singleness*. Cambridge: Grove.

_____. 2010. *Redeeming Singleness: How the Storyline of Scripture Affirms the Single Life*. Wheaton, IL: Crossway.

Dawn, M. J. 1993. *Sexual Character: Beyond Technique to Intimacy*. Grand Rapids, MI: William B. Eerdmans Publishing Company.

DeYoung, K. 2015. *What Does the Bible Really Teach about Homosexuality?* Wheaton, IL: Crossway.

Gagnon, R. A. J. 2001. *The Bible and Homosexual Practice: Texts and Hermeneutics*. Nashville: Abingdon.

Harrison, G. 2016. *A Better Story: God, Sex and Human Flourishing*. IVP.

Hiestand, G. L. and Wilson, T., eds. 2017. *Beauty, Order, and Mystery: A Christian Vision of Human Sexuality*. IVP Academic.

Jones, B. F. 2015. *Faithful: A Theology of Sex*. Zondervan.

Owens, T. M. 2015. *Embracing the Body: Finding God in Our Flesh and Bone*. IVP.

Slattery, J. 2018. *Rethinking Sexuality: God's Design and Why It Matters*. Multnomah.

Sprinkle, P. 2015. *People to be loved: Why homosexuality is not just an issue*. Zondervan.

Vines, M. 2014. *God and the Gay Christian: The biblical case in support of same-sex relationships*. New York: Convergent Books.

Volf, M. 1997. *After our likeness: The Church as the image of the Trinity*. Grand Rapids, MI: Wm. B. Eerdmans Publishing Company.

West, C. 2018. *Theology of the body for beginners: Rediscovering the meaning of life, love, sex, and gender*. North Palm Beach, FL: Beacon Publishing.

Wilson, T. 2017. *Mere sexuality: Rediscovering the Christian vision of sexuality*. Zondervan.

Yuan, C. 2018. *Holy sexuality and the Gospel: Sex, desire, and relationships shaped by God's grand story*. Multnomah.

Practical Application

Allberry, S. 2015. *Is God anti-gay? And other questions about homosexuality, the Bible and same-sex attraction*. The Good Book Company.

Allender, D. A. and Longman, T. 2014. *God loves sex: An honest conversation about sexual desire and holiness*. Grand Rapids, MI: Baker Publishing House.

Baker, D. 1984. *Beyond forgiveness: The healing touch of church discipline*. Portland, OR: Multnomah Press.

Baldock, K. 2014. *Walking the bridgeless canyon: Repairing the breach between the Church and the LGBT community.* Canyon Walker Press.

Bartlett, L. 2014. *The Failure of Sex Education in the Church: Mistaken Identity, Compromised Purity: Questions & Answers for Christian Dialogue.* Titus 2 for Life.

Barton, R. H. 1998. *Equal to the task: Men and women in partnership.* IVP.

Bennett, D. 2018. A war of loves: *The unexpected story of a gay activist discovering Jesus.* Zondervan.

Benyei, C.R. 2005. *When a congregation is betrayed: Responding to clergy misconduct.* Rowman & Littlefield Publishers.

Brooks, T. 2019. *Precious remedies against Satan's devices.* Puritan Paperbacks.

Carnes, P. and Moriarity, J. 1997. *Sexual anorexia: Overcoming sexual self-hatred.* Center City, MN: Hazelden.

Chan, F. and Chan, L. 2014. *You and me forever: Marriage in light of eternity.* San Francisco: Claire Love Publishing.

Cloud, H. and Townsend, J. 1992. *Boundaries: When to say yes, when to say no to take control of your life.* Zondervan: Grand Rapids, MI.

Coakley, S. 2015. *The new asceticism: Sexuality, gender and the quest for God.* New York: Bloomsbury.

Cohn, R. 2011. *Coming home to passion: Restoring loving sexuality to couples with histories of childhood trauma and neglect.* Praeger.

Crabb, L. 2013. *Fully Alive: A biblical vision of gender that frees men and women to live beyond stereotypes.* Grand Rapids, MI: Baker Books.

_____. 2013. *The Marriage Builder: Creating True Oneness to Transform Your Marriage.* Zondervan.

Friberg, N. C. and Laaser, M. R. 1998. *Before the fall: Preventing pastoral sexual abuse.* Collegeville, MN: The Liturgical Press.

Gallagher, S.. 2000. *On the altar of sexual idolatry.* Dry Ridge, KY: Pure Life Ministries.

Grenz, S. 1990. *Sexual ethics: A biblical perspective.* Dallas: Word Publishing.

Grenz, S. J. and R. D. Bell. 1995. *Betrayal of trust: Sexual misconduct in the pastorate.* Downers Grove, IL: InterVarsity Press.

Gushee, D. P. 2017. *Changing our mind: Definitive 3rd edition of the landmark call for inclusion of LGBTQ Christians with response to critics.* Read the Spirit books.

Henson, B. 2018. Guiding families of LGBT+ loved ones. Posture Shift Books.

Hill, W. 2013. *Washed and waiting: Reflections on Christian Faithfulness and Homosexuality.* Grand Rapids, MI: Zondervan._____. 2015. *Spiritual Friendship: Finding Love in the Church as a Celibate Gay Christian.* Grand Rapids, MI: Brazos Press.

Isom, M. 2018. *Sex, Jesus, and the Conversations the Church Forgot*. Grand Rapids, MI: Baker Books.

Jones, S. and B. Jones. 2007. *God's design for sex: 4 books* (age related). NavPress.

Joy, D. M. 1986. *Re-bonding: Preventing and restoring damaged relationships*. Waco, TX: Word Books.

_____. 1988. *Parents, kids, & sexual integrity*. Waco, TX: Word Books.

_____. 1999. *Bonding: Relationship in the image of God*. Nappanee, IN: Evangel Publishing House.

Keller, T. and Keller, K. 2013. *The meaning of marriage: Facing the complexities of commitment with the wisdom of God*. Penguin Books Publishing.

Kreider, L. N.d. Guidelines for church discipline and restoration for partner church members. http://hillconsultinggroup.org/assets/pdfs/articles/discipline-restoration-members.pdf.

Langberg, D. M. 2003. *Counseling survivors of sexual abuse*. Xulon Press.

Laney, J. C. 1985. *A guide to church discipline*. Minneapolis: Bethany House Publishers.

Lee, J. 2013. Torn: *Rescuing the Gospel from the Gay vs. Christian debate*. Jericho Books.

Maltz, W. 2001. *The sexual healing journey: A guide for survivors of sexual abuse*. New York: HarperCollins Publishers.

McIntosh, G. L. and Rima, S. D. 1992. *Overcoming the dark side of leadership: The paradox of personal dysfunction*. Baker Books: Grand Rapids, MI.

Moore, B. 2002. *When godly people do ungodly things: Finding authentic restoration in the age of seduction*. Nashville, TN: Broadman & Holman Publishers.

Ormerod, N. and Ormerod, T. 1995. *When ministers sin: Sexual abuse in the churches*. Alexandria, Australia: Millennium Books.

Ott, K. M. 2009. Sex and the seminary: Preparing ministers for sexual health and justice. *Religious institute on sexual morality, justice, and healing*. New York: Union Theological Seminary in the City of New York.

Payne, L. 1995. *The healing presence: Curing the soul through union with Christ*. Grand Rapids, MI: Hamewith Books.

Pedigo, T. L. 2007. *Restoration manual: A workbook for restoring fallen ministers and religious leaders*. Colorado Springs, CO: Winning Edge Publication.

Roberts, V. 2016. *Transgender*. The Good Book Company.

Schaumburg, H. W. 1992. *False intimacy: Understanding the struggle of sexual addiction*. Colorado Springs: NavPress.

_____. 2009. *Undefiled: Redemption from sexual sin, restoration for broken relationships*. Moody Publishers.

Schoenborn, K. 2013.*Warrior wives: Marriage is worth fighting for*. Redemption Press.

Shaw, E. 2015. *Same-Sex Attraction and the Church: The Surprising Plausibility of the Celibate Life*. Downers Grove, IL: InterVarsity Press.

Sipe, A. W. R. 2003. *Celibacy in crisis: A secret world revisited*. New York: Brunner- Routledge.

Slattery, J. 2017. *Sex and the Single Girl*. Chicago: Moody Press.

Stringer, J. 2018. *Unwanted: How sexual brokenness reveals our way to healing*. NavPress.

Struthers, W. 2010. *Wired for intimacy: How pornography hijacks the male brain*. Downers Grove, IL: IVP.

Thoburn, J. and Baker, R., eds. 2011. *Clergy sexual misconduct: A systems approach to prevention, intervention and oversight*. Gentle Path Press.

Walker, A. T. 2017. *God and the transgender debate: What does the Bible actually say about gender identity?* The Good Book Company.

Walls, J. L., Neill, J., and D. Baggett, eds. 2018. *Venus and virtue: Celebrating sex and seeking sanctification*. Cascade books.

Wardle, T. 2017. *Identity matters: Discovering who you are in Christ*. Leafwood Publishers.

Weiss, D. 2002. *Sex, men and God*. Lake Mary, FL: Siloam Press.

White, J. 1977. *Eros defiled: The Christian & sexual sin*. Downers Grove, IL: InterVarsity Press.

_____.1993. *Eros redeemed: Breaking the stranglehold of sexual sin.*Downers Grove, IL: InterVarsity Press.

White, J. and Blue, K. 1985. *Healing the wounded: The costly love of church discipline*. Downers Grove, IL: InterVarsity Press.

Willard, D. 2002. *Renovation of the heart: Putting on the character of Christ*. Colorado Springs, CO: NavPress.

Wilson, E., Wilson, S., Friesen, P., Friesen, V., Paulson, L. and Paulson, N. 1997. *Restoring the Fallen: A team approach to caring, confronting and reconciling*. Downers Grove, IL: InterVarsity Press.

Wharton, K. 2013. *Single-Minded: Being single, whole and living life to the full*. Oxford: Monarch Books.

Wraight, H. 1987. Single: The Jesus model. Crossway Books.

Yarhouse, M. 2010. *Homosexuality and the Christian*. Bloomington, MN: Bethany.

_____. 2013. *Understanding sexual identity: A resource for youth ministry*. Grand Rapids: Zondervan.

_____. 2015. *Understanding gender dysphoria*. Downers Grove, IL: InterVarsity Press.

Yuan, C. and Yuan, A. 2011._*Out of a far country: A gay son's journey to God. A broken mother's search for hope*. Colorado Springs: WaterBrook Press.

Yuan, C. 2016. *Giving a Voice to the Voiceless: A Qualitative Study of Reducing Marginalization of Lesbian, Gay, Bisexual and Same-Sex Attracted Students at Christian Colleges and Universities*. Eugene, OR: Wipf & Stock.

Sex Education Resources

Balswick, J. K. and J. O. Balswick. 1999. *Authentic human sexuality: An integrated Christian approach.* Downers Grove, IL: InterVarsity Press.

Burns, J. 2008. *Teaching your children healthy sexuality: A biblical approach to preparing them for life.* Bloomington, MN: Bethany House Publishers.

Butler, B, Evert, J. and C. Evert. 2016. You. Life, love, and the theology of the body. (For teens. Leaders Guide, Student Guide, Parent Guide and 5-dvd set available). Ascension Press.

Concordia Publishing House has a series of books that are gender specific on sexuality. See https://www.cph.org/c-2910-learning-about-sex.aspx.

Fort, J. W. 2019. *Honest talk: A new perspective on talking to your kids about sex.* Garden Ridge, TX: Be Broken.

Holcomb, J. S. and Holcomb, L. A. 2015. *God made all of me: A book to help children protect their bodies.* Greensboro, NC: New Growth Press.

Jones, S. and Jones, B. 2007. *God's design for sex* (series for 3-5, 5-8, 8-11, and 11-14-year olds). NavPress.

Leman, K. 2002. *Sheet music: Uncovering the secrets of sexual intimacy in marriage.* Tyndale House Publishers, Inc.

Penner, C. and Penner, J. J. 2003. *The gift of sex: A guide to sexual fulfillment.* Thomas Nelson.

Rogers, J. 2019. *Yours is yours and mine is mine: When it's OK not to share.* T.A.L.K. Consulting.

Rosenau, D. E. 2002. *A celebration of sex: A guide to enjoying God's gift of sexual intimacy*. Thomas Nelson.

_____. 2012. Soul virgins: *Redefining single sexuality*. Sexual Wholeness Resources.

Sellers, T. S. 2017. *Sex, God & the conservative Church: Erasing shame from sexual intimacy*. Routledge.

Slattery, J. 2015. *25 questions you're afraid to ask about love, sex and intimacy*. Moody Publishers.

Smedes, L. B. 1994. *Sex for Christians.* Grand Rapids, MI: Wm. B. Eerdmans Publishing Company.

The body matters books (picture books through 8th grade). Find on https://tobet.org/product-category/bodymattersbooks/.

Other Resources:

https://bethesdaworkshops.org/ (Christian treatment for sex addiction)

https://cmda.org/transgender-and-sexual-orientation/ (Christian Medical and Dental Association position paper)

https://conquerseries.com/ (sexual addiction)

https://desertstream.org/living-waters/ (deeper discipleship, healing relational and sexual brokenness)

Gresh, D. Age appropriate books for girls. Age appropriate books for boys. Both series can be found on Amazon.

https://healingcare.org/ (Terry Wardle's deeper discipleship healing ministry)

https://puredesire.org/(developing sexual integrity)

About the Author

Dr. Lisa Sinclair is a licensed family nurse practitioner with certification in psychiatric mental health. She earned her Doctor of Ministry from Columbia Biblical Seminary in member care. She and her husband, Paul, served as missionaries in Mali, West Africa with United World Mission. She also knows what it means to be a pastor's wife in a megachurch context. She is a member care consultant and travels internationally providing workshops and counseling as a BrookLink facilitator (http://brooklink.org/). Her areas of expertise include grief, trauma, stress and sexuality. She is an adjunct professor with Columbia International University and the Wisconsin Center for Christian Study (https://www.wisccs.org/).

Dr. Sinclair is a frequent speaker at conferences and retreats. She serves on the board of the Congo Initiative (https://congoinitiative.org/) and the church council at Eastbrook Church (http://eastbrook.org/). She is involved in prison ministry through Brother Bob's Outreach (https://www.brotherbobs.org/). She loves to swim, watercolor, read, and play with her grandchildren and dog. She and her husband live in Glendale, Wisconsin.